TWO APPROACHES
TO TEACHING SYNTAX

Published for the

Indiana University English Curriculum Study Center

EDWARD B. JENKINSON, *Director*

TWO APPROACHES
TO TEACHING SYNTAX

By
MARSHALL L. BROWN
ELMER G. WHITE
EDWARD B. JENKINSON

Indiana University Press
BLOOMINGTON · LONDON

Copyright © 1967 by Indiana University Press

All rights reserved

Library of Congress catalog card number: 67-63016

Manufactured in the United States of America

CONTENTS

FOREWORD

If it is no longer fashionable to ask "Why teach grammar at all," it is not because the question has been answered to the askers' satisfaction, but because the askers have been intimidated. With so many grammars competing for the teachers' attention, the old question was pushed aside in favor of another, "Which grammar shall we teach?" While both of these questions await answers, a third question is being asked: "How shall we teach grammar?" But the basic question, the one upon which all the others depend, is seldom heard: "What is grammar?"

One of the merits of this book is the fact that it begins with a sensible definition of grammar: "Grammar, as we use the term, is the study of English sentences to determine how words are put together to convey meaning. Grammar, then, is the study of the structure of English sentences." The authors would be the first to admit that this book is not "a complete grammar"; they have learned from modern linguistics that grammar is a much larger and far more complex subject than the writers of the old one-volume complete grammars realized. They have also learned, as all good teachers must, that it is neither necessary nor desirable to teach all that one knows about a given subject. They have chosen —wisely, I think—to stress syntax, recognizing that syntax is not all of grammar, but insisting that it is what students need most to understand.

How one teaches grammar—or any other subject, for that matter —depends on what one takes that subject to be. If grammar is a small body of immutable rules about a mass of relatively inaccessible data, created by fiat and delivered by authority, and if the desired end is knowledge of those rules, then rote memorization probably makes sense. But if grammar is the study of one's own native language, if its rules are subject to immediate verification by reference to intuitive knowledge and readily accessible data, and if the desired end is understanding how one's language works, then another sort of teaching is clearly indicated. Our authors' approach to teaching grammar follows logically from their definition of the subject: it is commonly called inductive teaching.

At first glance inductive teaching may seem to be of two kinds: at one extreme lies programmed instruction, which leads through carefully selected and arranged data to a predetermined generalization; at the other extreme lies free inquiry, which begins with unsorted data and leads where it will. But the fact is that the two kinds are very closely related. Behind every programmed course lies free inquiry, which has discovered and mapped the way for later travelers. The value of the method lies not only in the final destination, whether it be called generalization, definition, or rule, but also in the road and the travel that lead to it. The authors of this book have naturally learned a great deal from those who have traveled ahead of them, from C. C. Fries to Noam Chomsky, but Messrs. Brown and White have also made the trip themselves, with many classes of junior and senior high school students. All three authors have benefited from the experience of teachers in the pilot schools who have tested these two approaches to grammar in their own classes and suggested useful revisions.

The answer to the question "Which grammar shall we teach" also depends upon what one takes grammar to be. If grammar is, as the authors of this book define it, "the study of English sentences to determine how words are put together to convey meaning," then that grammar is best which exposes not only the structure of sentences, but also the construction of sentences. The key words here are "put together." Some grammars regard language as something to be taken apart to see how it works; what seems to be needed is a grammar that regards language as something that one puts together to see how it works. Such a grammar can take advantage of the everyday practice and intuitive knowledge of native speakers, whose use of language necessarily involves putting pieces together in order to convey meaning. The kind of grammar that is concerned with how verbal structures become what they are, as well as with what they are, is called transformational-generative grammar. It is that grammar that this book is about.

For most school teachers of English the important question is still the old one, "Why teach grammar at all?" It is, in one sense, a cry of despair. Research has failed to prove that the older grammar made better readers and writers of their students; and champions of the newer grammar often give answers which, if not simply embarrassing, seem to ignore what teachers still regard as the basic issue. Why teach grammar? Because it is exciting, says the linguist; because it is beautiful, because it is a fascinating subject in its own right. But teachers, perhaps even those who have got some glimpse of the beauty and the fascination, are far from certain that their students will agree.

The writers of this book, as teachers of English, are concerned about the practical, as well as the aesthetic, side of their subject. Despite dire warnings against it,* they have mixed a bit of rhetoric with their approaches to grammar, and without apologies. They are convinced these two approaches to grammar will be more useful than the old grammar was, and a recent bit of research suggests that they may well be right. A report published by the National Council of Teachers of English has shown that "a knowledge of generative grammar enables students to increase significantly the proportion of well-formed sentences that they write . . . [and] can enable students to reduce the occurrence of errors in their writing."†

More research of this sort will be forthcoming. In the meantime, prospective teachers of these two approaches to grammar will be interested in reports from the pilot schools where they have been taught. "My students tackle English sentences with enthusiasm and interest," says one teacher. Another teacher, working with slow learners, writes: "To be able to *discover* a sentence pattern N V$_{tran}$

---

*E. G., by James B. McMillan, "A Philosophy of Language," in Harold B. Allen, ed., *Readings in Applied Linguistics,* Second Edition (New York: Appleton-Century-Crofts, 1964), p. 286.

†Donald Bateman and Frank Zidonis, *The Effect of a Study of Transformational Grammar on the Writing of Ninth and Tenth Graders* (Champaign, Illinois, 1966), p. 39.

N_{io} N_{do} made them feel ten feet tall. When a class of underprivileged students . . . got excited about the basic structure of the English sentence, I felt ten feet tall, too." Perhaps the linguists have a point after all.

WILLIAM H. WIATT
Associate Professor of English
Indiana University

ACKNOWLEDGMENTS

The portion of the project of the Indiana University English Curriculum Study Center reported herein was supported through the Cooperative Research Program of the Office of Education, U.S. Department of Health, Education, and Welfare.

The IU Center received additional financial support from the Cummins Engine Foundation, which awarded Indiana University a grant that provided funds for meetings and equipment that could not be financed by the grant from the U.S. Office of Education.

The staff of the Indiana University English Curriculum Study Center wishes to thank William E. Wilson, former State Superintendent of Public Instruction, and Edgar B. Smith, former Assistant Superintendent of Public Instruction, for launching this project in 1962 by appointing teachers to committees to help develop the courses of study and by appointing Edward B. Jenkinson, Coordinator for School English Language Arts at Indiana University, chairman of the committees. The staff further wishes to thank the State Department of Public Instruction, under the direction of Richard D. Wells, Superintendent, for distributing this volume to all junior high school teachers of English in Indiana's public schools.

Many teachers and students played important roles in shaping this volume by contributing ideas, by making suggestions for revisions of various sections of the two grammars, and by experimenting with these approaches to grammar in their classrooms. They painstakingly helped to eliminate errors from the various drafts. The writers accept responsibility for the errors that remain.

The writers are especially indebted to Dr. Thomas Wetmore, Chairman of the Department of English, Ball State University, and to Dr. Ruth Strickland, Research Professor of Education, Indiana University, for their close reading of the manuscript.

In the early stages of the English Curriculum Study Center, a committee met periodically on the campus of Indiana University to make plans for a program in syntax. Members of the state-appointed Committee on Language that helped formulate those plans include:

Miss Ruth Bertsch, Teacher of English, North Central High School, Indianapolis.
Harold Garriott, Associate Professor of English, DePauw University
Miss Frances Graybill, Chairman of the Department of English, Paoli High School
Sterling Jackson, Teacher of English, New Trier High School, Winnetka, Illinois
Mrs. Joyce Reed, Chairman of the Department of English, Fremont Consolidated School
Webb Salmon, Director of Freshman Composition, Florida State University, Tallahassee
Owen Thomas, Associate Professor of English, Indiana University
Mrs. Margaret Walker, English Coordinator, Hammond Public Schools
Thomas Wetmore, Chairman of the Department of English, Ball State University

The following teachers who were appointed to the Committee on English for Slow-learning Students also helped to plan this volume:

J. R. Bishop, Teacher of English, Franklin Community High School
Eugene A. Campanale, formerly Director of Secondary Education, Marion Public Schools
Mrs. Ethel Campbell, formerly Chairman of the Department of English, Central Junior-Senior High School, South Bend
Sister Francis de Sales, C.S.C., Teacher of English, Bishop Noll Institute, Hammond
Mrs. Susie Dewey, Supervisor of English, Vigo County Public Schools
Mrs. Furniss Holloway, Teacher of English, Crispus Attucks High School, Indianapolis
Mrs. Annette Houston, Teacher of English, Seymour High School
Mrs. Dorothy Lewis, Teacher of English, Clarksville High School
Miss Muriel Ryall, Teacher of English, New Albany High School

The staff of the English Curriculum Study Center also received invaluable suggestions from these teachers who taught the grammars in their classrooms:

Mrs. Helen Ashworth, formerly Teacher of English, Mt. Vernon Junior High School
Mrs. Frances Blake, Chairman of the Department of English, Franklin Community High School

Acknowledgments

Mrs. Sharon Buell, Teacher of English, Brazil Senior High Sc
Mrs. Jeanne Campbell, formerly Teacher of English, Noblesvin.
School
Mrs. Betty DeVol, Teacher of English, Warren Central High School, ı.
apolis
Mrs. Margaret Dillard, Teacher of English, Franklin Community High School
Mrs. Mary Dold, Chairman of the Department of English, Portage High School
Miss Sandra Sue Dragoo, Teacher of English, Lakeside Junior High School,
Fort Wayne
Miles D. Eley, Teacher of English, Warren Central High School, Indianapolis
Mrs. Marjorie Foster, Teacher of English, Northside Junior High School,
Columbus
Mrs. Mary Ruth Fowler, Teacher of English, Warren Central High School,
Indianapolis
Mrs. Florence Fox, formerly Teacher of English, Franklin Community High
School
Miss Fay Hadley, formerly Teacher of English, River Forest Junior High
School, Hobart
Mrs. Jean M. Hawley, Teacher of English, Mt. Vernon Junior High School
Charles Hayden, Teacher of English, Huntington County Community High
School
James Hedges, Teacher of English, Mt. Vernon High School
Mrs. Maryanne Hertzer, formerly Teacher of English, Warren Central High
School, Indianapolis
Mrs. Gloria Hjerpe, Teacher of English, William A. Wirt School, Gary
Mrs. Ruth Homco, formerly Teacher of English, River Forest High School,
Hobart
Miss Catharine L. Howard, Chairman of the Department of English, Mt.
Vernon High School
Mrs. Olive Hughey, Teacher of English, Franklin Community High School
Mrs. Ernestine Humphreys, Chairman of the Department of English, Glenn
Junior High School, Terre Haute
Miss Mabel Hunter, Chairman of the Department of English, Oliver P. Morton
High School, Hammond
Miss Catherine Jackson, Chairman of the Department of English, Central High
School, Fort Wayne
Malcolm Julian, Supervisor of English and Foreign Languages, Muncie City
School System
Miss Karen Kenyon, Teacher of English, Franklin Community High School
Virgil Kirkpatrick, formerly Teacher of English, Warren Central High School,
Indianapolis
James Larcomb, Teacher of English, William A. Wirt School, Gary
Mrs. Evelyn Lindsey, formerly Teacher of English, River Forest Junior High
School, Hobart
Miss Lois McClure, Teacher of English, Huntington County Community High
School
Mrs. Judy McKinney, Teacher of English, Tipton High School
Miss Arlene Miller, formerly Teacher of English, River Forest High School,
Hobart
Mrs. Isabelle Morris, Teacher of English, Noblesville Junior High School

Mrs. Daphene Morrison, Teacher of English, Joseph P. Tuttle Junior High School, Crawfordsville
Mrs. Neva Mount, Teacher of English, Tipton Junior High School
Mrs. Mona Paulson, Teacher of English, Central Junior-Senior High School, South Bend
Fredrick Preston, Teacher of English, Central High School, Muncie
Mrs. Elizabeth Reilly, Chairman of the Department of English, West Vigo High School, West Terre Haute
Mrs. Betty M. Smith, Teacher of English, Penn High School, Mishawaka
Mrs. Viola Soderstrom, Teacher of English, River Forest High School, Hobart
Miss Marguerite Taylor, Teacher of English, Garfield High School, Terre Haute
Mrs. Carol Wheeler, formerly Teacher of English, Aylesworth Junior High School, Portage
Mrs. Annie Wilkerson, Teacher of English, Beckman Junior High School, Gary
Fred E. Wolfe, Teacher of English, Wilson Junior High School, Muncie
Mrs. Juanita Young, Chairman of the Department of English, Huntington County Community High School

The staff of the English Curriculum Study Center is especially grateful to Professor Philip B. Daghlian, Department of English, Indiana University, and Professor William H. Wiatt, Department of English, Indiana University, who spent many hours discussing the volume with the writers and making invaluable suggestions. Both Professor Wiatt and Professor Ingrid Strom, of the School of Education at Indiana University, also experimented with the materials in their college classrooms.

The units in this volume have undergone many revisions, each of which had to be typed, mimeographed, and mailed to pilot-school teachers. Three secretaries—Mrs. Robert Spencer, Mrs. James Louden, and Miss Donna Holtel—cheerfully accepted the tasks of retyping the many revisions and of proofreading the final volume.

THE GRAMMAR OF ENGLISH SENTENCES

An Approach to Syntax for Teachers of Talented and Average Students in Grades Seven Through Nine

By

MARSHALL L. BROWN

Teacher of English, Culver Military Academy

and

ELMER G. WHITE

Teacher of English, Culver Military Academy

with EDWARD B. JENKINSON, *Contributing Editor*
Coordinator for School English Language Arts and
Director of the English Curriculum Study Center
Indiana University

Introduction

In this program we aim to give teachers in grades seven through nine a meaningful treatment of elementary sentence structures.* By encouraging teachers to let students examine a large number of English sentences to discover how words work in sentences, we hope to reinforce the considerable amount of intuitive knowledge of the English language that junior and senior high school students already have.

That intuitive knowledge of English presents one of the major difficulties in teaching or in studying grammar. Both the teacher and the student, in one very important sense, already "know" a great deal about their own language. By the age of six, native speakers of English have mastered the handful of basic English sentence patterns. By the time a child enters junior high school, he employs a wide variety of English sentences, even though he may be unaware of his ability to do so. Only rarely, however, can a student discuss sentences in any meaningful way. And one of the purposes of studying grammar is to permit the student and the teacher to talk about their language in such a way that the student gains insights into the nature of language and, ideally, applies those insights to improve his own use of language.

The fact that we "know" so much about our language, even before we begin to discuss it, makes the selection of a starting place difficult. That knowledge also makes it difficult for us teachers to refrain from attempting to teach our students all that we know about syntax instead of teaching them only what they need to know to understand how words work in everyday sentences. This pro-

*Our task was to prepare a sequence in syntax for grades seven through nine. By testing this program in pilot schools, we found that the sequence can be taught in grades four, five, and six, as well as in junior high school.

2

gram, for reasons which will become obvious as the various steps unfold, begins by distinguishing between form words and structure words, and it limits itself to aspects of syntax that students can understand and can apply to their own sentences—both oral and written.

One major assumption underlying the presentation of this pedagogical grammar is that, in the study of language, inductive teaching is preferable to either deductive or prescriptive teaching. That is, the student should be led to form his own generalizations where possible. Instead of defining terms for the student, the teacher should encourage the student to establish classes of words and then to form his own definition of each class after he has examined many sentences to see how words work. However, in any classroom in which language is being discussed, a teacher will sometimes want to draw specific observations from certain generalizations; or to put the matter another way, on the basis of certain generalizations inductively arrived at, the teacher will formulate certain rules about the behavior of the English language.

As the teacher reads this program in grammar, we ask him to assume the roles of both teacher and student for two reasons: (a) to become familiar with aspects of grammar which are, in one sense or another, "new"; (b) to become acquainted with one inductive approach to teaching grammar—an approach which, we think, will help students understand and retain grammatical concepts and also help them to apply those concepts in their written and oral composition.

We also ask the teacher to answer the questions and complete the suggested exercises which, for the most part, have been tested in different grades with students of various academic abilities. Since we have tested this material in different classrooms, we feel that we can suggest, from time to time, specific approaches and exercises which, we found, help the diligent student to better understand how words work in English sentences.

The approach that follows does not pretend to be a complete grammar, a textbook, or a series of daily lesson plans designed to tell the teacher exactly what to do on any given day. Instead, this program is a course of study designed to give teachers a description of one approach to the grammar of English sentences.

Grade Seven

Before a student begins the study of any subject, he should have a good idea of what it is that he is going to study and why he is being asked to study it. In the past, many students left English classes with, at best, only a fuzzy notion of why they studied grammar. And many left classes wondering what grammar is.

The term *grammar* has become so all-inclusive that it has literally lost its meaning for many people. One grammarian summarized attitudes toward the term *grammar* very well when she noted: "The word *grammar* is public property; it has lost any special, technical sense it once may have had. To some, it is the name for the body of information about language—the terms, the rules, and so on. To others, the word has something to do with linguistic hygiene. To still others, *grammar* is what remains of the study of English after literature, rhetoric, and public speaking have been drained off—the dregs of the course."*

Since grammar means so many things to different people, we feel that it is necessary for students to understand exactly what it is that they are going to study before they begin studying it. Perhaps the teacher will want to ask students to define grammar before he gives a definition that applies to this program. The students' responses should illustrate quite graphically that the word itself has no meaning; people have given many meanings to the word. (See the unit on the dictionary for grade seven in *What Is Language?*, a volume in this English Curriculum Study Series.) Grammar, as we use the term, is the study of English sentences to determine how words are put together to convey meaning. Grammar, then, is the study of the structures of English sentences.

*Josephine P. Lowery, *This Is Grammar* (New York: Charles Scribner's, 1965), p. 1.

4

We will begin our study of grammar by focusing on different classes of words so that students can distinguish between classes before they begin examining sentences. In every step in this program, we hope to take advantage of the intuitive knowledge as well as of the classroom knowledge of English that the student already has. And we further hope to show the student that he can apply the knowledge that he has acquired in the study of grammar to improve his written and oral composition.

FORM WORDS
AND STRUCTURE WORDS

The English sentence is composed of five groups* of form words (sometimes called class words) and five groups of structure words (sometimes called function words). To help students see the difference between form words and structure words, the teacher may write words like these on the chalkboard:

goat   appear   gay

After writing those words on the chalkboard, the teacher may ask questions like these:

1. What meanings have men given to each of those words? (Students who have already studied the unit, "So What's a Dictionary For?" in the volume *What Is Language?* in this curriculum series, will understand why the question is "What meanings have men given to each of these words?" instead of "What do these words mean?") Can you give a synonym for each word?
2. If you read the words in the order that they appear on the chalkboard, do you feel that they almost form a sentence? If so, why? (By the time students enter the seventh grade they have heard the term *sentence* so many times and have attempted to define it so frequently that we feel that we

---

*Some linguists classify nouns, pronouns, verbs, adverbs, and adjectives as form words. Although it is easy to quarrel with the placement of adverbs in the category of form words, we will simply refer to the five groups and emphasize only nouns, verbs, and adjectives as form words.

dare risk using the term without calling undue attention to it or defining it at this stage.)

3. What letters (or sounds) can you add to each of the words and still have a recognizable word? (Students should have little difficulty adding the graphemes -*s* to both *goat* and *appear* and -*er* and -*est* to *gay*. Note that our question asks what letters or sounds can be added. To be linguistically correct, we would first be concerned with the phonemes— smallest meaningful units of sound—that could be added to the words before we would consider the graphemes— smallest meaningful units of writing. To make students aware that letters of our alphabet represent sounds, and not vice versa, we will frequently list the phonemes that can be added as well as the graphemes which represent those phonemes. In the case of the words *goat* and *appear*, we add the phonemes /s/ and /z/, and to *gay* we can add the phonemes /ər/ and /əst/.)

After asking those questions, the teacher may wish to put words like these on the chalkboard:

the   of   some   should   very

Again, the teacher may ask the same questions that he asked about "goat appear gay." Students probably had little difficulty answering the questions for the first group of words—"goat appear gay"; but they probably found that they could not answer the same questions for the second group of words—"the of some should very." Why? What are the differences between the two groups of words? The first group—"goat appear gay"—represents the classes of words that function as the "meat" of a sentence. In proper order they come close to making a sentence, if only of a Pidgin-English variety.* Here are other groups of form words that come close to making sentences:

desk   look   neat
man   feel   cold
dog   chase   cat

---

*In proper order and with the proper affixes, those words can make a good English sentence, e.g., goats appear gay.

Each of those groups gives us the feeling of a sentence, but we do not feel the same way about the following groups of words:

a   the   has   very
each   with   all of the   had

If we ask students whether those two groups of words give them the feeling of sentences, they will probably answer no. Asked to arrange the words in orders that would better give them the feeling of sentences, they might come up with arrangements like these:

the ____ has a very ____
each ____ had all of the ____ with ____

Orderings similar to those above are as close as we can come to producing sentences with words from the second group. Students should be led to see that words in the first group (desk look neat, and so on) can form a Pidgin-English sentence that does make sense to them, whereas words in the second group (the a has very, and so on) can only form the basic frame, or structure, of a sentence. Hence, we call them structure words.

Now let's focus on form words to lead students to see three classes—nouns, verbs, and adjectives.

First we will consider the word *goat* that appeared in the group of words, "goat appear gay." We have already seen that we can add the phoneme /s/ or the grapheme -s to goat to produce its plural form. What else besides /s/ or -s can we add to *goat?* To get students to discover what else can be added to *goat*, we might ask questions like these:

1. If we are writing, what do we add to *goat* if we want to talk about its tail?
2. If we are writing, what do we add to *goat* if we want to talk about the tails of more than one goat?

The answers to those questions should lead students to see that we have, in writing, four basic forms of the word *goat:*

goat   goats   goat's   goats'

(Note to the teacher: At this stage, for the sake of convenience, we shall refer to the added letters only as endings. In later units in

the language study program [see the volume *What Is Language?*],
students will become acquainted with the terms affixes, prefixes,
suffixes, and morphemes.)

What other words can students think of that can have the same
endings as *goat?* Students should have little difficulty providing the
teacher with a long list of words that form their plurals, in writing,
by adding -*s* and their possessives by adding -'*s* and -*s*'.

After students have discussed the endings that can be attached
to *goat* and other similar words, they should consider the word
appear. What are the typical endings that can be added to *appear*
if we write it? To help students answer that question, we might ask
them to fill in the blanks with an appropriate form of *appear* in
sentences like these:

> The girl will _____.
> The girl _____.
> The girl _____ yesterday.
> The girl is _____ now.

These, then, are the four basic forms of *appear:*

> appear   appears   appeared   appearing

Are the endings for *appear* the same as those that we added to
goat? Since they are not, is it reasonable to conclude that *goat* and
appear can be said to belong to different classes of words? (Of
course, the grapheme -*s* can work with both words, but whereas
goats means more than one goat, *appears* does not mean more than
one appear.)

After students have considered the endings for the words *goat*
and *appear,* they should consider the word *gay.* The teacher may
wish to have students fill in the blanks with the appropriate forms
of *gay* in sentences like these:

> Sally is _____.
> Sally is _____ than Sue.
> Sally is the _____ girl in our class.

The basic forms of *gay* are:

> gay   gayer   gayest

Now we should ask students whether the graphemes *-er* and *-est* can be attached to either *goat* or *appear?* Can the endings that we attached to *goat* be added to *gay?* Can the endings that we added to *appear* be added to either *goat* or *gay?* Students should immediately recognize that the answers to all those questions are no. The fact that each of those words takes different endings indicates that each belongs to a different class.

There is a second way to distinguish among the types of form words. Students should consider the word *goat* as it appears in a sentence like this:

_____ goat eats tin cans.

What words can students put before *goat?* They should come up with a list of words like this:

the	every	his
a	some	Joe's
one	that	this
each	any	our

If we add *-s* to goat and change the sentence to

_____ goats eat tin cans.

then students should see that they can place words like these in front of goats:

three	several	these
two	only	those
all	many	the

The question to ask at this point is: "Under normal circumstances, can we place those words that we have placed in front of *goat* in front of *appear* and *gay?*"

Next we might ask students what words can normally precede *appear* in its basic forms. We might ask students to fill in the blanks in sentences like these:

1. The actor _____ appear in a new movie.
2. The actor _____ appearing in a new movie.
3. The actor _____ appeared in a new movie.

For (1) students should have listed words like these:

will   would   should   may   can   might

For (2) students should have given words like these:

is   was   should be   might be

And for (3) students may have volunteered words like these:

has   had   should have   would have

Students probably thought of other words that could be put in
the blank for (1), since there are combinations of two or more of
those words listed that can be used. We will work with combinations of auxiliaries later. But now we can be content if our students
understand that the English language contains words that are
typically used with words like *appear* but not normally used with
words like *goat* and *gay*.

Finally, we should look for some examples of structure words
that normally precede a word like *gay*. Students may be asked to
fill in the blanks in sentences like the one below with as many different single words as they can:

Sally seems _____ gay.

They should have used words like these:

very   rather   somewhat   quite

Again, these words do not normally precede *goat* and *appear*, but
they can precede *gay*.

Thus far students should have discovered two important ways in
which three groups of form words are different from one another:
(a) Each class of form words has its own typical endings; (b) Each
class of form words can be preceded by specific kinds of structure
words.

To simplify our work, we should give names to the different
kinds of form words and define them in terms of the data that we
have discovered so far.

The word *goat* (and any word that can be treated in the same
way) is called a noun. On the basis of what students have just

learned about words like *goat*, we can ask them to write a descriptive definition of *noun*. If they fail to give a reasonable definition, we can supply a descriptive definition like this:

> A noun is one of the classes of form words. In general, it can
> a. have *-s*, *-'s*, or *-s'* attached to its simple written form;
> b. be preceded by such structure words as *the, a, some, every, one, this*, and so forth.

We call the word *appear* (and words that can be treated in the same way) a verb. Students should be able to write a descriptive definition of *verb* in terms of the data they have observed. If they fail to give a reasonable descriptive definition, the teacher can supply one like this:

> A verb is one of the classes of form words. In general, it can
> a. have *-s*, *-es*, *-ing*, or *-ed* attached to its simple written form;
> b. be preceded by such structure words as *will, should, is, had*, and so forth.

We call the word *gay* (and any word that can be treated in the same way) an adjective. As with the noun and the verb, students should be asked to write their own descriptive definitions of *adjective* in terms of the data they have examined so far. If they fail to produce a reasonable descriptive definition, the teacher can supply one like this:

> An adjective is one of the classes of form words. In general, it can
> a. have *-er*, or *-est* attached to its simple written form;
> b. be preceded by such structure words as *very, somewhat, quite*, and so forth.

The three types of structure words that we have referred to so far are called *determiners, auxiliaries*, and *qualifiers*. The structure words that work with nouns are called *determiners;* the structure words that work with verbs are called *auxiliaries;* and those that work with adjectives are called *qualifiers*.

Now let's have students find a third difference among form words. By writing sentence frames like those below on the chalkboard, we should be able to show students that the different classes of form words occupy different positions in sentences. Have students consider the following:

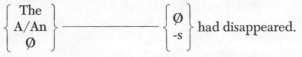

$$\left\{ \begin{array}{c} \text{The} \\ \text{A/An} \\ \varnothing \end{array} \right\} \underline{\hspace{3cm}} \left\{ \begin{array}{c} \varnothing \\ \text{-s} \end{array} \right\} \text{had disappeared.}$$

(The braces indicate that the writer or speaker has a choice of elements to use. The Ø, or null sign, shows that he can choose to use nothing at all. The element that he does choose depends upon the specific word that he puts in the blank.)

Ask students which of the three kinds of form words we have considered so far will fit into the blank above. They should note that the noun is the only one that fits into the blank, and by examining several test sentences written on the board, they should conclude that, typically, the first position in a basic sentence is occupied by a noun and its determiner.

Next, students should fill in the blank in a test sentence like this:

$$\left\{ \begin{array}{c} \text{Someone} \\ \text{Something} \end{array} \right\} \text{is} \underline{\hspace{3cm}}\text{-ing.}$$

Which of the three types of form words will fit into the blank? The verb, of course. Typically, the second position in a sentence is occupied by the verb or by the verb and its auxiliary.

Finally, students should consider a test sentence like this:

Something seems very _____.

Which of the three types of form words will fit into that blank? The adjective. But note that we cannot say an adjective usually fills the third position in a sentence. However, we can say that adjectives typically follow verbs like *seems* and *appears* and qualifiers like *very, rather,* and *somewhat.*

If a student memorizes the sentences we have just examined, he will have a handy test for determining which form class a given word belongs to. After examining such test sentences, a student should also realize that more complete descriptive definitions of *noun, verb,* and *adjective* might also include a statement on the positions that each typically occupies in the test sentences.

NOUNS AND THEIR PLURALS

Few academically talented and average students in grade seven cannot form the proper plurals of nouns. Although they do not realize that they add the phonemes /s/, /z/, or /əz/ to nouns in their conversation to form the plurals, they probably do so without making many errors. But when it comes to writing, they may have difficulty adding the proper graphemes. But even in writing, seventh graders have already formed some generalizations and they would probably be insulted if the teacher were to ask a question like this: "Do all nouns form their plurals by adding -*s*?" But even though seventh graders know the answer to that question, they still need some review in forming the written plurals of nouns.

Instead of giving students rules, the teacher can have them examine words and form their own rules from their generalizations. For example, the teacher may wish to put seven groups of words like these on the chalkboard:

book	church	goose	cherry	sheep	alumnus	ox
table	dish	foot	library	deer	alumna	child
school	birch	woman	baby	people	basis	

By asking students how the words in each group form their plurals, the teacher can get them to generalize about words that are similar to those listed on the chalkboard and thus students can form their own rules which will probably be similar to these:

1. Most nouns simply add the grapheme -*s*.
2. Some nouns like *dish* and *church* add the graphemes -*es*.
3. Some nouns like *goose* and *woman* form their plurals by internal changes in the word. Thus, we have plurals like *geese, women, teeth,* and so on.
4. Words ending in the grapheme *y* preceded by a consonant change the *y* to -*i* and add -*es*.
5. Some nouns like *sheep* and *deer* retain the same form in the plural.
6. Nouns that have been borrowed from Latin or Greek may retain their Latin or Greek plurals and thus seem highly irregular. For instance, *alumnus,* the singular, becomes

alumni; alumna becomes *alumnae; thesis* becomes *theses;* and *basis* becomes *bases.*

7. Two words in English, *ox* and *child,* form their plurals by adding *-en* or *-ren,* thus becoming *oxen* and *children.*

ADJECTIVES

Earlier we noted that one of the distinguishing features of the adjective is that it can usually add, in writing, *-er* and *-est* to form its comparative and superlative degrees. (Earlier we did not note that those forms are called comparative and superlative, and we are not convinced that students need to know that they are called comparative and superlative so long as they use them properly.) But not all adjectives form their comparative and superlative degrees by adding *-er* and *-est.* Words that fit into the blank for the adjective in this test sentence

Something seems very _____.

fit into one of four categories:

     a. Those words which can have *-er* and *-est* added to them; for example, *lovely, lonely,* and *wise.*

     b. Those words which cannot have *-er* and *-est* added to them; for example, *beautiful, patriotic,* and *loyal.*

     c. Those words which may add *-er* and *-est* or which may be preceded by *more* and *most;* for example, *lovely, lovelier* or *more lovely, loveliest* or *most lovely;* and *lonely, lonelier* or *more lonely, loneliest* or *most lonely.*

     d. Those words which form their comparative and superlative degrees irregularly; for example, *good, better, best,* and *bad, worse, worst.*

FORM WORDS
WITH MULTIPLE IDENTITIES

Does a given word belong to one class and only one class of words? In other words, if students call a word a noun, must it always remain a noun in sentences or can it function as a member of another class of words? To show students that one word may work in various ways, we can use the critical parts of the test sentences from page 12.

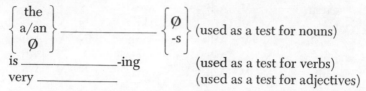

(used as a test for nouns)

is _____-ing   (used as a test for verbs)
very _____   (used as a test for adjectives)

Students may arrive at an answer to that question by trying to put various words into those blanks. For example, each word in the list below may be tried in each of the test sentences above. Students should label each word as N, V, or Adj, according to the test blank(s) that it fits.

test	smell	sew	match
water	thin	axe	fail
light	row	run	fair

After students have attempted to fit those words into different test frames, they should be able to generalize that sometimes one word may work in various capacities in English sentences.

Practice in Identifying Form Words

Here, again, are the test frames for identifying nouns, verbs, and adjectives:

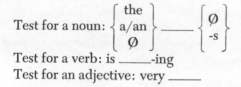

Test for a verb: is _____-ing
Test for an adjective: very _____

Students should be asked to try each word in a list like that given below in each of the test frames above. The teacher may wish to mimeograph such a list and have students circle the symbol or symbols to show into how many test frames each word can fit.

show	N V Adj		eat	N V Adj
ocean	N V Adj		box	N V Adj

steam	N V Adj	brave	N V Adj
serious	N V Adj	speed	N V Adj
fire	N V Adj	goat	N V Adj
catch	N V Adj	wealth	N V Adj
beg	N V Adj	slow	N V Adj
touch	N V Adj	game	N V Adj
funny	N V Adj	march	N V Adj
smile	N V Adj	love	N V Adj

If students have difficulty identifying form words, the teacher may wish to give them an exercise like the one below in which they fill blanks with nonsense words. To fill the blanks properly, students cannot rely on meaning for clues but must rely entirely upon their knowledge of affixes, structure words, and word order.

As students fill in each of the blanks with the nonsense words that are immediately beneath each sentence, they should tell for each blank whether the nonsense word functions as a noun, a verb, or an adjective.* They should also note that some of the words may not fit into any of the blanks, and they should be able to explain why some nonsense words do not fit.

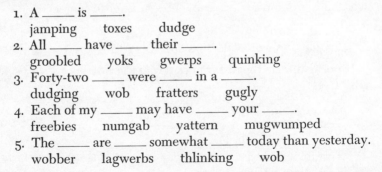

1. A ____ is ____.
   jamping   toxes   dudge
2. All ____ have ____ their ____.
   groobled   yoks   gwerps   quinking
3. Forty-two ____ were ____ in a ____.
   dudging   wob   fratters   gugly
4. Each of my ____ may have ____ your ____.
   freebies   numgab   yattern   mugwumped
5. The ____ are ____ somewhat ____ today than yesterday.
   wobber   lagwerbs   thlinking   wob

After students have completed this exercise, the teacher should review the sentences, asking questions that will make students

---

*There is a high degree of probability that most students will complete the first sentence like this: "A dudge is jamping." But one student may insist on "A jamping is dudge," which could be translated as "A beating is necessary." The teacher, then, should be prepared to accept sentences that students can defend.

aware that they chose words to fill the blanks because of word endings, word order, sentence positions, and structure words. Thus, if students filled the blanks with words they could defend, they know a great deal more about the structure of their language than they think they do.

REGULAR VERBS

With the exception of the verb *be*, verbs fall into two classes: regular and irregular. (*Be* is so irregular that it forms a separate class.)

Beginning with verbs like *appear*, teachers can get students to arrive at generalizations about regular verbs by asking questions like these:

1. What form of the verb *appear* do we use in a sentence like this: "I _____ whenever mother doesn't want me"?
2. What form of *appear* do we use in a sentence like this: "He usually _____ whenever there is no work to do"?
3. What form of *appear* do we use to express simple past action? Or to put the question another way, what form of *appear* do we use in a sentence like this: "Yesterday he _____ at the picnic"?
4. What form of *appear* do we use in a sentence like this: "He keeps _____ whenever we do not want him"?
5. What form of *appear* do we use when we precede *appear* with forms of the auxiliary *have*? Or to put the question another way, what form of *appear* do we use in a sentence like this: "The boy has _____ regularly since last Sunday"?

Students should note that, according to its endings, a verb like *appear* has four distinct forms: *appear, appears, appearing,* and *appeared.* The last form, *appeared,* works both in simple past tense and in sentences in which *appeared* is preceded by *have* or *has.* Verbs like *appear* are said to be regular because they have four distinct forms, and because they form both their past tense and their past participle by adding the graphemes *-ed.*

To give students practice before they make their own generalizations about regular verbs, the teacher might put verbs like these on the chalkboard with these column headings:

BASE FORM	THIRD PERSON PRESENT SINGULAR (WITH HE)	*-ing* FORM	PAST FORM	PAST PARTICIPLE FORM (PRECEDED BY A FORM OF HAVE)
walk				
burn				
work				
delay				
perform				

After students put the various forms of the different verbs under the column headings, the teacher should ask them to draw conclusions about regular verbs. Students should realize that regular verbs form their third person present tense, i.e., the form that is used with he, by simply adding *-s;* their *-ing* form by simply adding *-ing* to the base form; and both their past-tense form and past participle form by adding, in writing, the graphemes *-ed* to the base form.

IRREGULAR VERBS

Many English verbs do not form their past tense and past participle forms simply by adding the graphemes *-ed*. Students have been aware of these irregular verbs from the time they began talking and began having their parents correct them whenever they said something like this: "We singed the song yesterday." To make students aware of the irregular verbs, the teacher might put verbs like these on the chalkboard with five different column headings:

BASE FORM	THIRD PERSON PRESENT SINGULAR (WITH HE)	*-ing* FORM	PAST	PAST PARTICIPLE FORM (PRECEDED BY A FORM OF HAVE)
eat				
sleep				
run				
take				
sing				
see				

Students should readily see that there are several different ways that verbs form their past and past participle forms. There is no short cut to learning the various forms of the irregular verbs; students simply have to memorize those that they use most frequently. But instead of having students memorize a long list of irregular verbs, the teacher could probably help the students much more by giving them several irregular verbs each week during the seventh grade and by having them list the proper forms under each of the column headings as we have just done.

Some irregular verbs do fall into patterns; e.g., ring, rang, rung, and sing, sang, sung. But students must learn that they cannot fit a verb like *bring* into that same pattern by analogy.

THE VERB *BE*

The verb *be* is the most irregular verb in the English language. Other irregular verbs, as we have noted, have these five forms:

break   breaks   breaking   broke   broken

But the verb *be* has eight forms which students can learn for themselves by filling the blanks in the following sentences with one form of be:

1. You will _____ here.
2. I _____ here today.
3. He _____ here today.
4. You _____ here today.
5. Yesterday I _____ here.
6. Yesterday you _____ here.
7. We are _____ watched.
8. We have _____ watched.

These, then, are the forms of *be,* in the order in which they fit into the blanks above:

be	was	} (past form)
am	were	
is	being (present participle form)	
are	been (past participle form)	

MORE ABOUT VERBS

Before they can profitably examine elementary sentence structures, students must know more about verbs. To get students to
recognize one more feature of the verb, we might take them
through a series of steps like these:

1. the boy slept

After the teacher has written "the boy slept" on the board, he might
ask students: "Do you want to begin that group of words with a
capital letter? Why? Do you want to put a period after that group
of words? Why? Would you call that group of words a sentence?
Do you need to add something after the verb? If so, is the word,
or group of words, that you added a noun, an adjective, or a verb?"

After students have answered those questions, the teacher might
put a word-group like this on the chalkboard:

2. the boy seemed

Do students want to capitalize the word *the* in that group of
words? If so, why? If not, why not? Do they want to put a period
at the end of the group of words? If so, why? If not, why not? Do
they want to call that group of words a sentence? If not, why not?
Do they want to add something after the verb? What kind of word
do they want to add, i.e., a noun or an adjective? Do they feel that
they must add something after the verbs? Why?

After students have answered those questions, they are ready for
the third step.

3. the boy sold

Do students want to capitalize the word *the?* If not, why not? Do
they want to put a period after sold? If not, why not? Do they want
to call this group of words a sentence? If not, why not? Do they
feel that they must add a word after sold? If so, what kind of form
word must they add?

Now we can go back through the three groups of words and
make some generalizations about each group.

We need not add any more words to the first group. We *may*, if
we wish, add words like *soundly* or *in a tent*, or *late*, which looks

like an adjective, but we do not have to. And we certainly cannot add a noun, verb, or adjective (except *late*, which looks like an adjective) immediately after the first word-group. If we try to add one of those form words, we get nonsense like this:

The boy slept apple. (noun added)
The boy slept glad. (adjective added)
The boy slept sing. (verb added)

Most native speakers of English feel that one or more words need to be added to the second group—"the boy seemed." And most native speakers would add either a noun or an adjective, such as these:

The boy seemed a genius.
The boy seemed angry.

Most native speakers would also add at least one word to the third word-group—"the boy sold." And most native speakers would add a noun or a pronoun, such as:

The boy sold a telescope. (We must also consider that at least one student might add a particle, i.e., "The boy sold out," or a pronoun, i.e., "The boy sold it.")

From those groups of words, we can draw these conclusions: (a) Some verbs, like *sleep,* need not be followed by other words. (b) Some verbs, like *seem,* are almost always followed by either a noun or an adjective. (c) Some verbs, like *sell,* are almost always followed by a noun.

At this stage, the teacher will probably want students to form their own groups of words, using verbs like *sleep, seem,* and *sell.* After students have formed a number of sentences using verbs like those mentioned above, they may begin wondering if those verbs do not have names. And when students demand a name for a class of words, it is time to supply it to them since we know they will probably remember the name much longer than if we were to give it first and then describe the class. Therefore, we can give them this information, or better, we can ask them to arrive at generalizations that would lead to these terms: (a) A verb like *sleep,* which normally needs nothing to follow it, is called an *intransitive* verb. (b) A verb like *seem*, which must be followed by a noun or by an adjective, is called a *linking* verb. (c) A verb like *sell*, which is normally followed by a noun, is called a *transitive* verb.

One important point needs to be made here. We cannot look at any verb and declare it to be transitive, intransitive, or linking any more than we can look at a word like *light* and declare it to be only a noun, verb, or adjective, whichever term occurs to us first. Before putting any verb into a particular class, we need to put it into sentences. And after we have used it in different kinds of sentences, we may find that one verb can function in one sentence as an intransitive verb and in another sentence as a transitive verb.

WORD RELATIONSHIPS

A verb establishes relationships between words in a sentence. For example, in the sentence

The boy is a genius.

is connects the nouns *boy* and *genius,* both of which refer to the same person.

In the sentence

The boy seemed angry.

seemed connects the adjective *angry* with the noun *boy*. In this case the adjective *angry* describes the noun *boy*.

In the sentence

The boy sold his telescope.

sold does not connect *telescope* with *boy* in the same way that *seemed* connects *boy* with *angry* or *genius*. In the sentence, "The boy sold his telescope," *telescope* refers to something different from *boy*.

Relationships between the noun preceding the verb and the words following the verb offer one way of telling whether a verb is a linking or transitive verb. There is also a second way to tell whether a verb is a linking verb.

In the sentence

The boy seemed a genius.

we can cross out the verb and set off the second noun with commas like this:

The boy, a genius, (then we can complete the sentence).

In the sentence

The boy seemed angry.

we can cross out the verb and put the adjective before the noun like this:

The angry boy (then we can complete the sentence).

In changing "The boy seemed a genius" and "The boy seemed angry," we did not distort the meanings of the original sentences. But we cannot change this sentence:

The boy sold the telescope
       to
The boy, a telescope,
       or
The telescope boy . . .

Both of the above are unacceptable utterances.

Thus, we have learned that by striking out a verb that stands between two nouns (or a pronoun and a noun), we can determine that the verb is a linking verb if the second noun refers to the same person or if the adjective that follows the verb describes the noun that precedes the verb.

Again let's consider whether a given verb can function as more than one kind of verb. On the basis of what we have done so far, we can consider these sentences:

1. The man types.
2. The man types a letter.

In (1) is the verb intransitive, linking, or transitive? How can a student be certain? In (2) is the verb intransitive, linking, or transitive? How can a student be certain? What can he do to prove that the verb is transitive?

In (1) the verb is intransitive since nothing is needed to follow *types*. In (2) the verb *types* is transitive since it is followed by a noun that does not refer to *man*. Therefore, we can say that *type* is potentially either an intransitive or transitive verb. But before we could say this, we had to try the verb in at least two sentences. We cannot let our students forget that they cannot say that verbs are transitive or intransitive without first trying them in several sentences to see how they actually work in sentences.

Verb-phrase Exercise

The teacher may wish to give students an exercise like the one below in which they are asked to pick out the verb phrases. Students should be reminded that a verb phrase may consist of *one word* as well as of several words, including a noun phrase following the verb. Students should also tell whether each verb phrase is intransitive, linking, or transitive.

1. One of the girls ran.
2. Sally has become our secretary.
3. His uncle is reading yesterday's newspaper.
4. The general scolded one of his lieutenants.
5. Each pilot may fly this plane.
6. That lemonade looks good.
7. My father runs a store.
8. Each bird may fly.
9. Aunt Lou's pies are too sweet.
10. The coach seemed anxious.
11. The gardener grew petunias.
12. The coach grew weary.

THE BASIC SENTENCE

Thus far we have established some notions about the following items:

Form words (noun, verb, adjective)
Structure words (determiner, auxiliary, qualifier)
Affixes (those which are used as characteristic endings for form words)
Intransitive, linking, and transitive verb phrases

With these items we can build *basic* sentences, and with basic sentences we can, in turn, build compound and complex sentences.

To establish in the minds of students what we mean by *basic* sentences, we can refer them to this sentence:

The boy slept.

How many form words does it contain? To what classes do the form words belong?

In that sentence we have only a noun and its determiner followed by a verb. We need to add nothing else. Nor can we take anything away and still have a sentence. Therefore, we can say that "The boy slept" contains only essential elements and is a *basic* sentence.

In basic sentences we can say that each form word in the sentence occupies its own typical position. The noun normally occurs in the first position, and the verb in the second position. Students have also learned that there are three kinds of verbs: intransitive, linking, and transitive. They also know, from the test sentences that we have used, that there are three basic positions in our basic sentences. The first position contains the noun that precedes the verb; the second position is occupied by the verb; and the third position may be occupied by a noun or an adjective that follows the verb. Students should be reminded of the way of checking a form word that follows the verb to see whether it is a noun or an adjective. (See page 12.)

For the sake of expediency, we represent nouns, verbs, and adjectives by rather simple symbols, such as the following:

Noun	N
Intransitive verb	V_{intr}
Linking verb	V_{li}
Transitive verb	V_{tr}
Adjective	Adj

Now we should be able to use those symbols to represent, in shorthand fashion, these four types of basic sentences:

$N + V_{intr}$
The boy slept.

$$N + V_{li} + \left\{ \begin{array}{l} N \\ Adj \end{array} \right.$$
The boy is a genius.
The boy seemed angry.

$N + V_{tr} + N$
The boy sold his telescope.

$N + V_{tr} + N + N$
The boy sold John his telescope.

Each of those sets of symbols can represent a great number of sentences. For example, the set—$N + V_{intr}$—can represent sentences like these:

> The bat flew.
> A cow sleeps.
> Cats purr.
> The sun shines.
> The car stopped.

We say that sets of symbols like $N + V_{intr}$ represent the basic sentence *patterns*. The symbols are like recipes that tell us what ingredients to use in sentences. And since the recipes for basic sentence patterns are so important, students will find it helpful in their study of grammar to fix these patterns firmly in their minds:

Pattern 1: Dragons snarl.
$$N + V_{intr}$$

Pattern 2: The girl is a genius.
The girl is pretty.
$$N_1 + V_{li} + \begin{cases} N_1 \\ Adj \end{cases}$$
We have given subscript numbers to N to indicate that both nouns refer to the same person or thing.

Pattern 3: The boy hit the ball.
$$N_1 + V_{tr} + N_2$$
In this pattern the subscript numbers indicate that each noun refers to a different person or thing.

Pattern 4: Each girl knitted her mother a scarf.
$$N_1 + V_{tr} + N_2 + N_3$$
In Pattern 4 each of the three nouns refers to a different person or thing.

Basic Sentence Pattern Exercise

The teacher may wish to give students an exercise like the one below. Students should underline each form-word phrase and write its appropriate symbol below it.

Example: *A boy bought some apples.*
$$N_1 \quad V_{tr} \quad N_2$$

1. Some pilots crashed their planes.
2. That rock looks heavy.
3. Mr. Azimuth has become our chief.
4. The principal gave those students their awards.
5. This glass of lemonade tastes quite sour.
6. Every one of his friends should have applauded.
7. The horse has been trotting.
8. A salesman sold the housewife a sweeper.
9. The acrobat seems somewhat dizzy.
10. Cows eat grass.

WRITING BASIC SENTENCES

Given the basic sentence patterns, students should be able to write a number of different sentences for each pattern. In each of their sentences, they should try to use different form-word phrases, and they should, wherever possible, use powerful verbs that vividly describe the action.

$$N + V_{intr}$$
$$N_1 + V_{li} + N_1$$
$$N + V_{li} + Adj$$
$$N_1 + V_{tr} + N_2$$
$$N_1 + V_{tr} + N_2 + N_3$$

FORM-WORD PHRASES

Now we can consider, in somewhat more detail, the structure of the form-word phrases—that is, the word-groups built around nouns, verbs, and adjectives.

Thus far we have seen that each kind of form word has its own typical sets of affixes and structure words to be used with it. Our job now is to see in what ways nouns, verbs, and adjectives are formed into phrases varying from the simple to the complex.

THE NOUN PHRASE

The simplest noun phrase occurs in a sentence like this:

Joe growls.

Can we say that a sentence containing only two words, a noun and a verb, actually has a noun phrase as one of its parts? If we think back to the test-blank for the noun, we can see that even a single noun can be called a noun phrase.

$$\left\{ \begin{array}{c} \text{the} \\ \text{a/an} \\ \emptyset \end{array} \right\} \underline{\hspace{3cm}} \left\{ \begin{array}{c} \emptyset \\ \text{-s} \end{array} \right\}$$

With each noun we put into the blank, we choose one of the elements within the braces. If we put a proper name into the blank, for instance, we will probably choose not to precede it with a determiner. And if we use a singular noun, we will always add the $\emptyset$ affix. Since such choices are just as real as those of picking actual determiners and affixes, the $\emptyset$ represents the *potential* of the noun to be so accompanied. Therefore, a single noun can be thought of as a phrase consisting of the noun itself together with a zero determiner and a zero affix, neither of which do we actually speak or write.

Building the noun phrase from its simplest to most complex form involves the use of determiners and combinations of determiners. A detailed description of the determiner system would become much too involved for junior high school students; therefore, we will limit our discussion of determiners to these two points: (a) "Determiner," as one of the kinds of structure words, includes many words that we have traditionally labeled as adjectives, possessive nouns and pronouns, and articles. (b) The word "of," used with determiners, produces what linguists refer to as the "recursive" aspect of English sentence structure—that is, the potential for a given kind of element to recur again and again. Example: each *of* the men *of* the first squad *of* that platoon.

In connection with (a) above, it might be helpful to have students look at some noun-phrases with the determiners underlined (shown in italics below):

Ø tables	*this* rug
the cat	*that* charity
a dog	*several* houses
some man	*my* car
third chance	*girl's* mitten
six hours	*John's* ear

Traditionally, the italicized words above (except for Ø) have different names, such as article, possessive pronoun, demonstrative pronoun, and so forth, and, traditionally, they have been considered to function as adjectives. But can we call them adjectives according to the definition we have established thus far? Can we attach the typical adjective affixes to them? Can we precede them with words like *very, rather,* and *somewhat?* Can we fit them into the adjective test-blank? No. Therefore, we do not choose to call those words adjectives but prefer to call them determiners.

So far we have limited ourselves to using one determiner before a noun. What are the possibilities of using combinations of determiners? The native speaker of English generally has little or no difficulty putting several determiners together, but it might be of some interest to note a few characteristics of the determiner in this respect. Below are some determiners:

the	each	third
a/an	his	some
one	all	our
two	this	Jane's
first	those	that
last	my	her

After the teacher has written such a list on the chalkboard, he may ask each student to select a noun in its singular form and put several determiners in front of it. Then the teacher will have the student use the same noun in its plural form and see how many determiners he can put in front of it. The teacher will ask questions like these:

1. Are there some determiners that exclude any or all others?
2. What are they?

3. If a student selects *the, a,* or *an* as the initial determiner, what other determiners can follow as second and third determiners?
4. Are there any determiners that must be preceded by *the, a,* or *an?*
5. Are there any determiners that must be preceded by determiners other than *the, a,* or *an?*

Now let's consider the use of the word *of* with determiners. Here are some examples:

one of those boys*
each one of your dogs
these two of your five hats

In each case, *of* serves as a connector which enables us to put together combinations of determiners which otherwise would not be possible. Each of the examples that we have given above can be called a complete noun phrase. In terms of structure we are content to say that each consists of a noun preceded by a string of determiners.

Of also enables us to use certain nouns as parts of noun phrases, and it is this use that gives us the *recursive* characteristic of the noun phrase. For example, we can see the recursive characteristic in the following:

each one of that group of five of the first squad of men
the last four of the pages of your book of quotations

Each of the above examples is *one* noun phrase capable of being put into any of the noun positions in the basic sentences. Actually, we could go on and on adding more and more noun phrases connected by the word *of.* Hence, the term *recursive*—recurring again and again in chain-like fashion.

THE VERB PHRASE

The verb phrase is much less flexible in its structure than the noun phrase. Just as the noun has certain structure words, called determiners, that may precede it, so the verb may be preceded by

---

*The teacher may point out that when such a phrase serves as the subject of a sentence, the verb agrees with the element preceding *of.*

its own set of structure words, which are called auxiliaries. We illustrate the two kinds of auxiliaries in a series of sentences starting with these:

Charles *has* gone home.
The water *had* receded.
All the men *have* shaved.

In each of those sentences, the main verb is preceded by a form of the verb *have*.

Next students should look at sentences like these:

Charles *was* going home.
The water *is* receding.
All the men *are* shaving.
My cousins *were* leaving.

In those sentences each of the verbs is preceded by a form of the verb *be*. *Have* and *be*, then, in addition to being main verbs in their own right, can also be used as auxiliaries.

What should we say about words like *may, shall, must,* and *might*? Those, too, can be used before verbs, but they themselves are not capable of being used as main verbs. We call them *modal* (from "mood," or "mode") *auxiliaries,* or, more simply, *modals*. We will return to modals later in this section. But first we will examine the structure of the verb phrase, beginning with the simplest case. The teacher may wish to have students examine sentences like these:

The boys swim.
All dogs eat.
Some parrots talk.

After students have examined those sentences, the teacher may wish to ask questions like these: What form of the verb appears in each case? What governs our choice of the verb? Is the noun preceding the verb in each sentence singular or plural? If there are no modals or auxiliaries present, can we use only a plural noun to precede the base form of the verb?

Now students should examine sentences like these:

The boy swim*s*.
The dog sleep*s*.
A parrot talk*s*.

In those sentences we have the base form of the verb with the *-s* affix added. Students should note that the nouns that precede the verb are singular. They should further note that if there are no modals or auxiliaries preceding the verb we can use nothing but a singular noun to precede the *-s* form of the verb.

Some grammarians like to point out that

if N + -s, then V + Ø (i.e., if the noun has *-s* added, then the verb has nothing added)
and
if N + Ø, then V + -s.

Are there other sentences in which we use one-word verbs? If students cannot think of them readily, we might supply sentences like these:

The boy swam.   The boys swam.
A dog slept.   All of the dogs slept.
A parrot talked.   Some parrots talked.

In each of the above sentences, the *-ed* (past) form of the verb appears, regardless of whether the preceding noun is singular or plural.

The next step, then, is to consider verb phrases containing a verb preceded by a single auxiliary. We can give students sentences like these:

A parrot is talking.   All the students were reading.
I am writing.   Some men are working.
That girl was sewing.

In each of those sentences, the last word is the main verb word. We might ask students questions like these: In what form does the verb appear? The forms of what verb are used as auxiliaries? Can we ever use the *-ing* form of a verb (as a main verb) without preceding it with a form of *be* as an auxiliary?

Next, we should have students examine sentences like these in which the verb phrases are underlined:

The soldiers *have marched.*
Bob Smith *has written a book.**
A mob *had broken the window.*

*Note that *a book* should be underlined since that noun phrase is a part of the verb phrase if the deep structure of a sentence can be symbolized as S → NP + VP.

What form does the main verb word have in each sentence? Forms of what verb appear as auxiliaries? In basic sentences of the types we have worked with so far, what form must the main verb take if it is preceded by a form of *have*? Can we use the past participle form as a verb if we do not precede it with a form of *have*?

Then we should have students consider these sentences:

> Men should work.
> Some parrots may talk.
> My cousin will leave.
> A little rain must fall.

What form does the main verb word have in each sentence? Each main verb in this set of sentences is preceded by a modal auxiliary. Are modals always followed by the simple form of the verb? Yes.

Below is a list of the most commonly used modals:

must	can	should
may	could	will
might	shall	would

The teacher may wish to have students use each of those modals in sentences of their own. After each student has completed his sentences, he should be able to tell what form of the verb must follow the modal.

Some modals consist of more than one word, such as the following:

> ought to
> forms of *be* + to, e.g., *is to* arrive, *were to* arrive, etc.
> forms of *have* + to, e.g., *have to* work, *had to* work, etc.
> forms of *be* + going to, e.g., *was going to* leave, etc.
> forms of *be* + about to, e.g., *am about to* leave, etc.

Now that we have examined the forms that verbs take when they are preceded by a single auxiliary, we can use more than one auxiliary to determine what form the verb takes.

> The army should be marching.
> Your dog might be sleeping.
> All the children will be waiting.

When we use all possible auxiliaries (modal, a form of *have*, and a form of *be*), we construct sentences like these:

> Sally must have been working.
> The army might have been fighting.
> A taxi was to have been waiting.

Students should be asked: "In what order do the auxiliaries occur? Do they always occur in the same order?" The teacher might encourage students to put the auxiliaries in several different orders to determine if other orders are possible.

Practice with Verb Forms—1

The teacher may wish to have students complete an exercise like the following, in which the appropriate forms of the verb are put under the column headings.

BASE FORM	-*ed* (PAST FORM)	-*en* (PAST PARTICIPLE FORM)
laugh		
have		
bear		
tear		
freeze		
shake		
lift		
wander		
do		
be		
write		
fight		
see		
climb		
sneak		
soar		
catch		
bring		
think		
take		

Practice with Verb Forms—2

After students have completed the first exercise, the teacher may wish to have them complete an exercise like this in which they fill the blanks with the appropriate form(s) of the verb indicated in parentheses. (Some blanks may be filled with more than one form of the same verb.)

1. Joe's uncle _____ to the rodeo. (go)
2. Your mother is _____. (run)
3. That glass will _____. (break)
4. Our team may be _____. (play)
5. My shirt has _____ torn. (be)
6. Margaret ought to _____. (study)
7. The snow might have _____ by then. (melt)
8. The crowd should _____ been _____ by now. (have, dance)
9. Each boy _____ about to _____ home. (be, run)
10. Four of our party _____ going to _____ for the tickets. (be, pay)

Practice with Verb Forms—3

After students have completed the second exercise, the teacher may give them an exercise like the following in which they are to fill blanks with a verb phrase containing the elements indicated. Students should be asked to use a different modal each time one is called for.

1. Five cats _____ in our yard. (Modal and appropriate form of *fight*.)
2. The collector _____ strange butterflies. (Forms of *have* and *find*.)
3. Those dogs _____. (Modal and appropriate forms of *be* and *growl*.)
4. A group of four children _____ for ice-cream cones. (Modal and appropriate forms of *have*, *be*, and *hope*.)
5. All the teachers _____ papers all night. (Possible forms of *correct*.)

THE ADJECTIVE PHRASE

At this stage there is little that we need to say about the structure of the adjective phrase. However, we can make these three points. (a) As we have already seen, an adjective in its simplest form may be preceded by structure words called qualifiers. The number of qualifiers is quite small, and students already know most of them, such as:

> very   somewhat   rather   quite · too

Rarely do two or more of those qualifiers work in combinations as determiners and auxiliaries do, but it is possible to have a sentence like this: "That dress is somewhat too expensive." (b) An adjective phrase occurs in only one basic sentence:

$$N + V_{li} + Adj$$

Of course the adjective phrase does occur frequently in expanded noun phrases in all simple sentences. (c) The *-er* and *-est* forms of adjectives occur only in complex sentences such as this one: "This candy is sweeter than that candy (is sweet)." Such a sentence results from transformational operations that combine two or more basic sentences. The eighth-grade section of this grammar deals with those operations in some detail.

FORM AND FUNCTION

Thus far we have been concerned primarily with the different forms, or shapes, of form words. We have said that a word can be called a noun rather than a verb or adjective because its form is different from those of the other two. For later work in grammar, however, it is important to know the *functions* of the phrases that these words can be built into.

We begin our study of functions by asking students to consider the basic sentence as a whole. Each basic sentence can be separated into two main parts: (a) The first part of the sentence is made up of a phrase containing a noun or a pronoun or a word that functions like a noun. We call this first part of a sentence the *subject*. (b) The rest of the sentence is made up of one or more phrases—one of which contains a verb—which tell us something about the subject or which tell what the subject is doing. We call this part of the sentence the *predicate*.

The simplest sentences can be very short. Here are some examples:

> Fish swim.
> Canaries sing.
> People talk.

The subject and predicate of each of those sentences consist of the simplest noun and verb phrases.

Now let's try to see the relationship between form and function by examining several sentences.

> 1. The boy slept.

This sentence, students may recall, is an example of what we called an intransitive-verb sentence since we need nothing to follow the verb phrase. We identify "the boy" as a noun phrase by virtue of its structure, or form. The word *noun,* then, is a label indicating a certain kind of form-word phrase. The noun phrase, "the boy," functions as the subject of the sentence. The word "slept" is a verb which needs nothing to follow it; therefore, we say that it functions *intransitively.* The form of a word does not depend upon its position in a sentence. But we can tell the function of a word or phrase only after we have seen it in a specific sentence.

The predicate parts of each of the next two sentences consist of more than just a verb phrase.

> 2. The boy *is a genius.*
>   predicate
> 3. The boy *seemed angry.*
>   predicate

How do the verbs function in those sentences? Since they can be followed by either a noun phrase or by an adjective phrase, and since the relationships pointed out on pages 22 and 23 hold true, both "is" and "seemed" serve a linking function.

The teacher might ask students what is the relationship between "the boy" (subject) in number (2) and "a genius." Obviously both words refer to the same person. The noun phrase, "a genius," refers back to the subject. In terms of function, we call "a genius" a *sub-ject complement*. Again, in (3), the adjective phrase "angry" refers to the subject. Therefore, it, too, functions as a *subject complement*.

Now students should examine this sentence:

4. The boy *sold his telescope.*
           predicate

How does the verb "sold" function? Before a student can answer that question, he should look at the rest of the predicate. What is "his telescope"? It is a noun phrase. Does it refer back to the subject or to someone or something different? Since the noun phrase "his telescope" refers to something different from the subject, we say that the verb "sold" functions *transitively*. After a transitive verb phrase, a noun phrase is said to function as the *object*.

After students have become sufficiently familiar with the noun phrase that functions as an object after a transitive verb, the teacher may wish to move to a sentence like this:

5. Each girl *knitted her mother a scarf.*
           predicate

Again we have a verb phrase functioning transitively. Following the verb phrase are two noun phrases, each different from the other and each different from the subject. What is the function of the noun phrase "the scarf"? If we leave the second noun phrase out of the sentence, we have

Each girl knitted _____ a scarf.

The sentence is now like (4); hence, "a scarf" functions as the ob-ject. What is the function of the second noun phrase, "her mother"? It tells us *for whom* each girl knitted a scarf. Such a noun phrase functions as the *indirect object*. Does an indirect object always tell *for whom* something is done? Before students answer that ques-tion, they might examine sentences like these:

Charlie sold *his friend* an alligator.
My uncle gave *the beggar* a dollar.

In those sentences the indirect object tells *to* whom something was done.

In summary, we can say these things: (a) The words *noun, verb,* and *adjective* are labels to indicate kinds of form-word phrases. The class of a form word is determined by the structure word and affixes that may accompany it. (b) The *function* of a given form-word phrase is determined by its position in a sentence and by its relationship to other phrases in the sentence.

Thus we could call a phrase like "the goats" a noun phrase in *form* because it has a determiner + goat + -s. We could also call a phrase like "is swinging" a verb phrase in *form* because it has an auxiliary + swing + -*ing*. But we cannot label the function of either the noun phrase or the verb phrase until we see them in a sentence. Perhaps we can clarify this distinction between form and function for students with sentences like these:

> *The cats* drank the milk.
> John has fed *the cats*.
> Susie gave *all the cats* some mittens.

In those sentences the italicized phrases are all the same in terms of form—noun phrases. But in each sentence the italicized phrase has a different function. In the first the noun phrase functions as the subject, in the second as the object, and in the third as the indirect object. Therefore, we can say that the form is the same for all three phrases but the function is different.

To illustrate further the differences between form and function, we can give students sentences like these:

> Willie *turned* at Main Street.
> The day *has turned* hot.
> Willie *may have turned* the key in the lock.

In those sentences the italicized portions are the same in terms of form; all are verb phrases. But they differ in function. The first verb phrase functions intransitively; the second functions as a linking verb; and the third functions transitively.

Form and Function Exercise

The teacher may wish to give students an exercise like the following in which students are asked to tell both the form and the function of the italicized and underscored words.

1. Your albino catfish *looks sick*.
2. Each of John's books *seems dull*.
3. The boy *gave his uncle a present*.
4. *Ringo likes pears*.
5. This cake *should taste very good*.
6. *Arthur* pulled *the little girl's pigtail*.
7. *The water had become rather cold*.
8. The glass *feels quite smooth*.
9. *A few students* cheered *their team*.
10. *Mr. Archer arrived* on time.

ADVERBIAL ELEMENTS

A basic sentence, consisting as it does of only essential elements, often does not convey as much information as we, the listeners or readers, want. For example, in the basic sentence, "They boy slept," we might want to know how he slept, where he slept, or how long he slept. In other words, we want to substitute specific information for the italicized words in these sentences:

> The boy slept *sometime*.
> The boy slept *somewhere*.
> The boy slept *somehow*. (or *in some manner*)

Of course the use of *sometime, somewhere,* and *somehow* is not restricted to intransitive-verb sentences as these sentences illustrate:

> The boy is a genius *sometime*. (linking-verb sentence)
> The boy felt hungry *somewhere*. (linking-verb sentence)
> The boy sold his telescope *sometime*. (transitive-verb sentence)
> The boy gave his mother a present *in some manner*.
> (indirect-object sentence)

The foregoing examples show that these *some* elements are optional in all the basic-sentence patterns. If we substitute other words for *sometime, somewhere,* and *somehow,* we may form sentences like these:

1. My brother runs *fast*. (somehow)
2. Bob read the newspaper *quickly*. (somehow)
3. Every bowler went *home*. (somewhere)
4. The magician vanished *then*. (sometime)
5. The secretary sat *here*. (somewhere)

After students have examined sentences like those above, the teacher might ask them whether the words that have been substituted for *sometime, somewhere*, and *somehow* are all of the same type. It would be valuable to take the sentences one at a time, examining the words *fast, quickly, home, then*, and *here*.

The word *fast* we have already learned to classify as an adjective since it can precede a noun. The word *quickly* comes from the adjective quick, with the affix *-ly* added. The word *home* would normally be classified as a noun, and the words *then* and *here*, which we have not yet classified, indicate time and place.

The point of our troubling students with an analysis of those words is to show them that the optional elements *sometime, somewhere*, and *somehow* can be replaced by *different* kinds of words. In general, we say that *sometime, somewhere*, and *somehow*, which show the possibility of our adding information not essential to the basic sentence patterns, perform the *adverbial function*. Therefore, *any* structure that can be substituted for *sometime, somewhere*, and *somehow* also performs the adverbial function. For example:

1. The boy slept *during the day*.
2. The boy slept *behind the wall*.
3. The boy slept *with his feet on the desk*.

Those sentences all contain noun phrases preceded by a *preposition*. In each case the noun phrase is a substitute for either *sometime, somewhere*, or *somehow*. In sentences 1, 2, and 3, the prepositions *during, behind*, and *with* are structure words which serve as connectors to show the relationship between the verbs and the following noun phrases.

Instead of giving students a list of prepositions to memorize, the teacher can have students start their own list of prepositions by having them fill the blank in this sentence with as many prepositions as they can.

A farmer looked _____ his car.

Prepositions that students may use to fill the blank include:

at	around	under	for
above	into	outside	after
behind	in	over	through
beyond	within	near	beside

After students have filled the blank with as many single words as they can, the teacher should explain that the preposition with its following noun phrase is called a *prepositional phrase*. Students should also learn that not all prepositions consist of only one word. To illustrate that point, the teacher might put sentences like these on the chalkboard:

1. We played in spite of the rain.
2. We ran because of a fierce dog.
3. Uncle John drove as far as Boston.

In spite of, because of, and *as far as* are all examples of compound prepositions which indicate relationships other than those expressed by *sometime, somewhere,* and *somehow. Because of* indicates a "for some reason" relationship; *in spite of* indicates a "despite some reason" relationship; and *as far as* indicates a "for some distance" relationship.

Developing a List of Prepositions

To help students develop their own lists of prepositions, the teacher may give them an exercise like the following in which they fill in the blanks with as many prepositions as they can. Students should be reminded that prepositions may consist of more than one word.

1. Little Alec played _____ his yard.
2. His sister slept _____ noon.
3. Their mother looked _____ the stairway.
4. Grandma dozed _____ lunch.
5. A group of students raced _____ the hall.
6. We canceled the game _____ the flood.
7. Mr. Smax built his house _____ lumber.
8. Our school bus whizzed _____ the corner.

Infinitive Phrases

Another structure that commonly functions as an adverbial is the infinitive phrase. For example:

Aunt Lou ran *to find her purse.*
Burke and Hare dug holes *to make money.*

In each case the italicized element consists of a noun phrase preceded by the base form of a verb which, in turn, is preceded by the word *to.* A "to + verb" structure is called an infinitive, and the "to + verb + noun phrase" structure is called an infinitive phrase. (The eighth-grade program will show that the infinitive phrase may be thought of as a reduction of an adverbial clause. As such, it lies beyond the scope of the present program; but because the infinitive phrase occurs as an adverbial so frequently, we included a brief discussion of it here.)

Number of Adverbials in a Sentence

The teacher may ask students if a sentence may contain only one adverbial. As native speakers of English, students know that they can insert more than one adverbial in any sentence, as the following sentences illustrate:

During the summer John went *home frequently.*
    (three adverbials)
In the afternoon John *always* goes *to the golf course as quickly as possible.* (four adverbials)

The teacher may wish to give students several basic sentences and have students add as many adverbs as they can without making the sentences cumbersome.

Position of Adverbials

To illustrate to students that adverbials may occupy various positions in a sentence, the teacher might put sentences like these on the chalkboard:

Angrily, John cranked the old car.
John *angrily* cranked the old car.
John cranked the old car *angrily.*

The examples show that adverbials have no definitely fixed positions in sentences as noun phrases and verb phrases do. Of course, not all adverbials can be placed at the beginning of sentences, nor can all be placed between a noun phrase and a verb phrase as we did with *angrily*. For example:

> *Fast* John drove the car.
> John *fast* drove the car.
> John drove the car *fast*.

The first two utterances are unacceptable to native speakers of English; only the last utterance, with the adverbial at the end, is acceptable.

By way of summary, we can say:

a. Adverbials are optional elements in a sentence.

b. Adverbials may be nouns, adjectives, infinitive phrases, or prepositional phrases used adverbially:
   1. adjective (fast, hard, slow)
   2. adjective + -*ly* (softly, quickly, slowly)
   3. noun (home, yesterday, today)
   4. adverbs (here, there, now, then)
   5. prepositional phrase (at the door, in front of the house)
   6. preposition (up, down, off, on)
   7. infinitive phrase (to catch a thief)

c. Adverbials furnish specific information related to these *some* elements:
   1. sometime
   2. somewhere
   3. somehow
   4. for some reason
   5. for some distance
   6. despite some reason

d. Adverbials frequently occupy terminal positions in sentences, but they *may* be placed at the beginning of, or within, sentences. (Students should be urged to place adverbials in sentences with care.)

e. More than one adverbial may occur in a sentence.

TRANSFORMATIONAL
OPERATIONS

We have briefly described the structures of phrases and of basic sentences. Now we are ready to consider methods of making alterations in sentence structures. Such alterations, generally speaking, proceed according to regular sets of steps. We transform the original sentence; hence, the term *transformational grammar*.

What follows is an examination of the elementary transformations involving just one basic sentence at a time. These are *simple* transformations. Those which involve combining elements of two or more basic sentences into one are *complex* transformations, to be dealt with at length in the eighth-grade program. In the present program we will concern ourselves with transformational steps which will yield the following: (a) sentences beginning with the expletive *there;* (b) sentences in imperative (command) form; (c) questions answerable with "Yes" or "No"; (d) questions requiring answers other than "Yes" or "No."

THE THERE-EXPLETIVE
TRANSFORMATION

As a first step in helping students to see how sentences are transformed, the teacher may wish to put pairs of sentences like these on the chalkboard:

Two satellites were orbiting the earth.
There were two satellites orbiting the earth.

Some geese are in the pond.
There are some geese in the pond.

A few men have been waiting for us.
There have been a few men waiting for us.

To help students understand what has occurred in the transformations, the teacher might first ask a question like this: Is there any feature that remains constant in the basic form of each sentence? (Each contains a form of *be,* either as an auxiliary or as the main verb. Also, the determiner in each subject noun phrase is an indefinite one. Here, the teacher may spend just a few minutes explaining the differences between definite and indefinite if the class seems to require such an explanation.)

A second question might be: How does the verb element(s) differ in the transform from the verb element(s) in the original sentence? (If a form of *be* occurs as the main verb, we find that it comes before the subject in the transform. If the verb phrase contains one or more auxiliaries, they are placed before the subject in the transform.)

A third question might be: What element is present in the transform that is not present in the basic sentence? (The word *there* has been added, and it stands at the beginning of the transform. The word *there* does not perform an adverbial function in the sentences above, and it is called an *expletive*.)

Exercise on the There Transform

After the teacher is certain that students understand what happens in the *there* transform, he may ask them to make *there* transforms of sentences like these:

1. A dog was barking all night.
2. Some policemen were at school today.
3. Four mechanics are repairing my car.
4. A barge is floating near the dock.
5. A few cows are straying past the creek.

(If students clearly understand that *there* sentences are transforms, they may, by transforming a number of sentences, learn to avoid errors in subject-verb agreement.)

THE IMPERATIVE (COMMAND) TRANSFORMATION

To introduce students to the imperative transformation, the teacher may put a sentence like this on the board:

You will go home.

The teacher might ask, "Can we remove a single word from that sentence and still have a recognizable English sentence?" By removing the auxiliary *will*, students will have this sentence:

You go home.

"You go home" is a command which can be further reduced by removing the *you* and leaving only:

Go home.

Eliminating both "you" and the auxiliary "will" gives us the most common form of the imperative. If we retain the "you," we have a somewhat more emphatic command, e.g., "You, go home." In writing, we can give even more strength to the imperative by using punctuation like this:

Go home!
You, eat your spinach!

Frequently, we use a variation of the imperative in conversation. Since the word "you" is very indefinite when more than one person is within hearing, we may say this:

Harry, go home right after work.

The implied "you" occupies the subject position in that sentence. "Harry" serves merely to get the attention of, or to designate, which "you" we mean. We address the sentence to the person named. Traditionally, a name used in this way is called a *noun of address*. In writing, a noun of address at the beginning of a sentence is followed by a comma. If the noun of address occurs internally in a written sentence, it is set off by commas. If it occurs at the end of a written sentence, it is preceded by a comma.

Making Imperative Sentences

The teacher might ask students to make imperatives out of the sentences below and to explain why certain elements were eliminated. Students should also be asked to consider the response of the person being commanded to both the original sentence and to its imperative reduction. How does a person react to a command? When are commands necessary? Can commands be given in other than imperative forms?

1. George, you should not do that.
2. You will stay after school.
3. You (had) better not go home now.

4. You will give me a nickel.
5. You should wash the dishes tonight.

THE QUESTION TRANSFORM

Most of the sentences that we speak and write are statements. But when there is something that we do not know, we usually ask a question. And many questions that we ask can be answered by either "yes" or "no." The relationship between the *yes-no* question and its statement form should be easy for students to detect.

To illustrate that relationship, the teacher might first put a sentence like this on the chalkboard:

My brother has dropped the ball.

The teacher might ask students a question like this: "Suppose that we do not know whether or not the brother has dropped the ball. What question would we usually ask?" Students will probably respond like this:

Has my brother dropped the ball?

And the answer to that question would be a simple "yes" or "no."

If we put the statement and the question together so that we can examine them, we can ask some pertinent questions about each.

Statement: My brother has dropped the ball.
Question: Has my brother dropped the ball?

Have we used the same words in both the statement and the question? Yes, but we should notice that they are not in the same order. If we put more statements and questions together, students can see whether the same relationships are present in all of the pairs.

Statement: John is going home.
Question: Is John going home?
Statement: Those ducks have flown a long way.
Question: Have those ducks flown a long way?
Statement: The librarian should have been stacking these books.
Question: Should the librarian have been stacking these books?

If we take time to show how each statement is put together, and then show how its corresponding question is put together, students will see that a regular set of steps can be followed to change a statement into a question. First, we have students look at the italicized verb phrases in sentences like these:

John *is going* home.
Those ducks *have flown* a long way.
The librarian *should have been stacking* these books.

We notice that each verb phrase has one or more auxiliaries in front of the main verb.

is going
Aux Verb

have flown
Aux Verb

should have been stacking
Modal Aux Aux Verb

Next, we have students look at the questions with the verb phrases italicized.

Is John *going* home?
Aux   Verb

Have those ducks *flown* a long way?
Aux   Verb

Should the librarian *have been stacking* these books?
Modal   Aux Aux Verb

What differences do we note between the questions and the statements? In each of the questions the auxiliary (if there is only one), or the first auxiliary (if there is more than one), has been removed from the verb phrase and placed in front of the subject. The teacher will want to make certain that students understand how yes-no questions are formed before they attempt the following exercise.

Practice in Forming Yes-No Questions

The teacher may wish to give students an exercise like the following in which each statement has a verb phrase containing one or more auxiliaries. The student should write a yes-no question for each statement.

1. That silly cat has eaten too many cookies.
2. My father is running in the race.
3. The John X. Tew Company will hold its picnic tomorrow.
4. Abdul's camel has been drinking water for a day.
5. Admiral Toxy could have done a good job.
6. For a week she had been reading my book. (Students should note that the adverbial, *for a week,* is moved to the end of the sentence in the question. They should also attempt to transform other statements that have introductory adverbials to see what happens to the adverbials in the questions.)

Next, students should write a statement for each of the following questions and be prepared to explain what happens to the verb phrases as they change the questions into statements.

1. Have you been driving a car for a year?
2. Is his lawn mower repaired?
3. Has Georgianna been baking turkey pies again?
4. Will your mother like your haircut?

MORE YES-NO QUESTIONS

Not all statements can be transformed into questions by placing the auxiliary or modal before the subject. Because many statements contain neither auxiliaries nor modals, a different transformational process must be followed. For example:

Statement: John hit the ball.
Question: Did John hit the ball?

Statement: Those ducks flew a long way.
Question: Did those ducks fly a long way?

Statement: The librarian stacked the books.
Question: Did the librarian stack the books?

In each question the word *did** occurs in front of the noun phrase that is the subject. And, in each question, the verb is changed from

---

*A more thorough treatment of the appearance or non-appearance of the forms of *do* in questions is presented in the eighth-grade program.

the past-tense form in the statement to the base form in the question. If the verb in the statement is in the past tense, the past tense of *do* is used in the question. We must use a form of *do* in our questions since these utterances are unacceptable in modern English although they were quite acceptable several hundred years ago.

Hit John the ball?
Flew those ducks a long way?
Stacked the librarian the books?

If the statement contains a present-tense verb like this:

John goes to Boston every month.

then the question contains a present-tense form of the verb *do*, like this:

Does John go to Boston every month?

Not all statements containing neither auxiliaries nor modals can be transformed into questions by using a form of the verb *do*. For example, these sentences

Each student is here.
A few of these apples are green.
John was in his yard.

cannot be transformed into acceptable questions containing a form of the verb *do*, since most native speakers of English would reject questions like these:

Does each student be here?
Do a few of these apples be green?
Did John be in his yard?

Instead, native speakers would accept these transformations of the statements:

Is each student here?
Are a few of these apples green?
Was John in his yard?

Thus statements that contain a verb phrase consisting only of a form of the verb *be* are transformed into questions simply by placing the form of *be* in front of the noun phrase used as the subject.

But statements that contain a form of the verb *have* and no auxiliaries or modals can be transformed into questions by putting a form of the verb *do* in front of the subject. For example:

Statement: Each student has his book.
Question: Does each student have his book?

Statement: A few of these apples have wrinkles.
Question: Do a few of these apples have wrinkles?

Statement: John had a parrot.
Question: Did John have a parrot?

We can also transform statements that contain a form of the verb *have* without auxiliaries or modals into questions without using a form of the verb *do*. For example:

Statement: Each student has his book.
Question: Has each student his book?

Statement: A few of these apples have wrinkles.
Question: Have a few of these apples wrinkles?

Statement: John had a parrot.
Question: Had John a parrot?

The first and third questions may be acceptable to some native speakers of English. The second question, however, might prove troublesome to most native speakers of English since they would prefer a question that starts with a form of the verb *do*. Therefore, we can conclude that given a statement with a form of the verb *have* and no auxiliaries or modals, we can always form a yes-no question by using a form of the verb *do;* but we cannot always form a yes-no question without a form of the verb *do*.

Exercise in Forming Yes-No Questions

The teacher might wish to have students transform statements like these into questions.

1. My niece goes to bed early.
2. Each of those tangerines has seeds.

3. The clerk went to the bank.
4. Your mother was here today.
5. His uncle bought several newspapers.
6. That car has a new tire.
7. Three campers swam the swift river.
8. The staple gun is full of staples.
9. Those books have been checked out.
10. That tomato could be rotten.
11. Senator Smith will go to Denver.
12. Several of these old hats were worn by generals.
13. The boys were here hours ago.
14. I am holding my breath.
15. Charley will have been traveling for a week by now.
16. We have had a good time.
17. We had a good time.
18. The rocket will be speeding to the moon.
19. Every one of the girls can cook good steaks.
20. Poor Doug doesn't know his lesson.

QUESTIONS THAT CANNOT BE ANSWERED BY "YES" OR "NO"

Many framers of questions are not seeking yes-no answers; therefore, they phrase their questions so that they will yield more information than a simple "yes" or "no." To show students how such questions are transformed from statements, the teacher may begin with a statement like this:

The man has gone *somewhere*.

The first step in changing that statement into a question is to place the auxiliary in front of the subject like this:

Has the man gone *somewhere*?

That process gives us a yes-no question, but it will probably not elicit an answer that will tell us exactly where the man has gone. To obtain that information, we need to ask a question like this:

Where has the man gone?

To transform the statement, "The man has gone somewhere," into the question, "Where has the man gone?" we first formed a yes-no question and then we substituted the word *where* for *somewhere* and placed *where* at the beginning of the yes-no question. These examples may clarify the process for students:

Statement: The soldiers marched *sometime*.
Yes-no Q: Did the soldiers march *sometime*?
           When did the soldiers march?

Statement: The students listened *for some reason*.
Yes-no Q: Did the students listen *for some reason*?
           Why did the students listen?

Statement: The football team played *in some manner*.
Yes-no Q: Did the football team play *in some manner*?
           How did the football team play?

Statement: Each fisherman has caught *something*.
Yes-no Q: Has each fisherman caught *something*?
           What has each fisherman caught?

After students have carefully examined the steps in transforming the statements into questions, they should be able to tell what happens in each sentence. They should also be able to follow the transformational process from statement to question when the *some* word appears in front of the verb, as in:

Statement: *Someone* was eating my pie.
Yes-no Q: Was *someone* eating my pie?
           Who was eating my pie?

That example follows the same process as the preceding examples since the statement contained an auxiliary. Given a statement without an auxiliary, we would follow a process like this:

Statement: *Someone* ate my pie.
Yes-no Q: Did *someone* eat my pie?
           Who did eat my pie?

Most native speakers of English would not say: "Who did eat my pie?" Instead, they would say:

Who ate my pie?

To form that question, we need not take the yes-no question process step. That is, we did not use a form of *do* in the final question, "Who ate my pie?" Thus we eliminate one step in transforming into questions statements that contain no auxiliary and a *some* word as the subject. Example:

Statement: *Someone* tells the truth.
Question: *Who* tells the truth?

QUESTIONS WITH WHOSE AND WHOM

To help students understand how questions beginning with *whose* are transformed, the teacher may write statements and questions like these on the chalkboard:

Statement: *Someone's* book fell off the desk.
Yes-no Q: (The yes-no question step is eliminated since the *some* element occurs in the subject position.)
Question: *Whose* book fell off the desk?
Statement: Joe picked up *someone's* book.
Question: *Whose* book did Joe pick up?

When the possessive form of a *some* element occurs at the beginning of a statement, we transform the statement into a question by substituting *whose* for the possessive form of the *some* element. When the possessive form of a *some* element occurs with a noun phrase in a position other than the subject, we substitute *whose* for the *some* element and move the entire noun phrase to the front of the question.

Students may need to see more examples in which we refer to the final question as a *wh-question* since all substitutes (except *how*) for *some* elements begin with *wh-*.

Statement: *Someone's* car was stolen.
Wh-Question: *Whose* car was stolen?
Statement: *Someone's* cat is lost.
Wh-Question: *Whose* cat is lost?
Statement: The boy found *someone's* dog.
Yes-no Q: Did the boy find *someone's* dog?
Wh-Question: *Whose* dog did the boy find?

Statement: The thief stole *someone's* ring.
Yes-no Q: Did the thief steal *someone's* ring?
Wh-Question: *Whose* ring did the thief steal?

To help students understand how questions beginning with *whom* are transformed, the teacher may put statements and questions like these on the chalkboard:

Statement: The boy helped *someone*.
Yes-no Q: Did the boy help *someone*?
Wh-Question: *Whom* did the boy help?

Statement: The boy turned to *someone* for help.
Yes-no Q: Did the boy turn to *someone* for help?
Wh-Question: *Whom* did the boy turn to for help?
                              or
                    To *whom* did the boy turn for help?

In the sentence, "The boy helped *someone*," the *some* element functions as the direct object; therefore, we substitute *whom* for the *some* element. In the sentence, "The boy turned to *someone* for help," the *some* element functions as the object of a preposition; therefore, we substitute *whom* for the *some* element. We substitute *who* for the *some* element only when the *some* element functions as the subject or as a subject complement.

SUMMARY OF STEPS
FOR QUESTIONS

To transform a statement containing an auxiliary verb into a yes-no question, we simply place the first auxiliary or modal at the beginning of the question, like this:

Statement: John will go hunting this afternoon.
Yes-no Q: Will John go hunting this afternoon?

To transform a statement containing no auxiliaries or modals into a yes-no question, we put the proper form of *do* at the beginning of the questions and change the main verb to its base form, like this:

Statement: John fishes every afternoon.
Yes-no Q: Does John fish every afternoon?

Statement: Marjorie found a dollar.
Yes-no Q: Did Marjorie find a dollar?

To transform a statement into a wh-question, we first transform the sentence into a yes-no question, and then we substitute the proper wh-word for the *some* element and put the wh-word at the beginning of the question, like this:

Statement: The team played well *sometime*.
Yes-no Q: Did the team play well *sometime*?
Wh-Question: *When* did the team play well?

If the *some* element is the subject and if the statement contains no auxiliary or modal, then we simply replace the *some* element with the proper wh-word to transform the statement into a question. For example:

Statement: *Someone* plays tennis like a professional.
Wh-Question: *Who* plays tennis like a professional?

Practice in Forming Questions

The teacher may wish to give students an exercise like this in which they transform the statements into questions. The presence of an italicized *some* element calls for a wh-question.

1. You have been acting *in some manner* lately.
2. Four of those big crows were sitting *somewhere*.
3. Four of those big crows were sitting on my fence.
4. The dog ate the bone.
5. That fireman plays cards all day.
6. That fireman plays cards *sometime*.
7. *Someone* has been sitting in my chair.
8. Miss Booth closed her window *for some reason*.
9. *Something* climbed up the telephone pole.
10. *Someone* might have been watching you.

COMPOUND ELEMENTS IN SENTENCES

In the strictest sense, sentences containing compound elements are not basic sentences. The eighth-grade program will show in more detail how compound elements result from transformational processes. But because such compounding occurs so frequently, we include a simplified presentation here.

The word *compound,* as we use it here, means more than one of the same kind of thing. We make use of compound elements in sentences to avoid repeating words needlessly. For instance, we can have two sentences like these:

Mary washes the dishes.   Sue washes the dishes.

In both sentences the entire predicate is the same, and we use that predicate to combine both sentences into one.

Mary and Sue wash the dishes.

By taking the subject noun phrase from each sentence and by joining them with *and,* we form a sentence with a compound subject. More examples follow:

This book is mine. That paper is mine.
This book and that paper are mine.

Students should note the change in the verb.

Each of the men swam. Some of the boys swam.
Each of the men and some of the boys swam.

Did the form of the verb change in that sentence? Why not?

And is not the only word that we can use to join sentence elements. For example:

Each of the men swam. Only some of the boys swam.
Each of the men swam but only some of the boys swam.

Here is an example of another joining-word:

John may jump. Bill may jump.
John or Bill may jump.

Thus far we have used the words *and, but,* and *or* to join parts of sentences, and we call those words conjunctions. A conjunction joining two or more elements of the same kind is called a *coordinating* conjunction.

Another kind of conjunction appears below:

My cousin will arrive. My aunt will arrive.
Either my cousin *or* my aunt will arrive.

In the last sentence two words are used as one conjunction. Other pairs of words work in the same way.

My cousin will not arrive. My aunt will not arrive.
Neither my cousin *nor* my aunt will arrive.

My cousin will arrive. My aunt will arrive.
Both my cousin *and* my aunt will arrive.

We can join two (or more) of any of the same parts of sentences with conjunctions. We can join noun phrases, verb phrases, noun phrases used as objects, and so forth. Given below are several examples:

The little boy played. The little boy sang.
The little boy *played and sang*. (compound verb phrase)

Each of his sisters bought a doll. Each of his sisters bought a ball.
Each of his sisters bought *a doll and a ball*. (compound noun phrase used as an object)

Jo cut the cloth slowly. Jo cut the cloth carefully.
Jo cut the cloth *slowly and carefully*. (compound adverbial)

Compound Elements Exercise

Given below are sets of sentences. In each set the same kind of element is repeated. The teacher may ask students to combine each set of sentences into one sentence by using coordinating conjunctions.

1. The boys flew kites. The girls flew kites.
2. These four books are interesting. Those pictures are interesting.
3. Jack Smith ran home. Jack Smith watched TV.
4. My brother played in the yard. My brother played in the house.

5. John gave his sister some popcorn. He gave his mother some popcorn.
6. The men will visit the hospital. Their wives will visit the hospital.
7. We delivered papers in the wind. We delivered papers in the rain.
8. All of the girls liked that book. Some of the boys liked that book.

After students have combined the sentences, they should be asked to substitute different coordinating conjunctions for the one they used. What difference in meaning do they get by using a different conjunction?

THE COMPOUND SENTENCE

In the last section we joined *parts* of sentences by coordinating conjunctions. We can also use such conjunctions to join sentences.

Jill washed the dishes. Jack swept the floor.
Jill washed the dishes, *and* Jack swept the floor.
Jill washed the dishes, *but* Jack swept the floor.

In the first set of sentences we merely state two facts. But in the second and third, the conjunctions serve to point out a relationship between the two. When we use *and,* we are simply joining two statements. When we use *but,* we point out a contrast.

Here are some other examples of compound sentences:

The soldier soon fell asleep. He was tired.
The soldier soon fell asleep, *for* he was tired.

Bill did not eat much. He did not sleep well.
Bill did not eat much, *nor* did he sleep well.

The teacher might ask students questions like these: What mark of punctuation occurs before a coordinating conjunction joining two whole sentences? In the last sentence, what changes in word order did we make after *nor?* Do we always make such changes with *nor?* Are there some conjunctions that we did not use in joining *parts* of sentences? What are they? Can they be used to join parts of sentences—or can they be used only to join whole sentences? Can we use *either . . . or* and *neither . . . nor* to join sentences? Can we use *both . . . and?*

Using Coordinating Conjunctions
to Join Whole Sentences

The teacher may ask students to join sentences like these with as many coordinating conjunctions as they can use.

1. Joe went swimming often. He liked the exercise.
2. My turtle eats bugs. He eats lettuce.
3. Joan rode home with Bo. She liked my car better.
4. Bo's car doesn't have seats. It doesn't have a top. (Use *nor* as the conjunction.)
5. The horse eats twice a day. It gets hungry.

Grade Eight

Review is necessary in a three-year program in grammar. But any review, we believe, should not only emphasize major concepts but should also add to the student's knowledge of grammar. Therefore, in the review presented here, we do not merely reexamine phrase structure and basic sentence patterns, but we present more information to help students fix those concepts in their minds.

BASIC SENTENCE PATTERNS

In grade seven students learned that basic sentences contain only essential elements, i.e., noun and verb phrases and, in the case of linking-verb sentences, either an adjective or noun phrase following the verb phrase. The four basic sentence patterns introduced in grade seven can be presented by sets of symbols like these:

Pattern 1: $NP^* + VP_{intr}$
That plant should grow.

Pattern 2: $NP_1 + VP_{li} + \begin{cases} NP_1 \\ Adj \end{cases}$
My brother is a doctor.
My brother is ambitious.
(We use the subscript 1 with the noun phrase to indicate that both phrases refer to the same person or thing.)

Pattern 3: $NP_1 + VP_{tr} + NP_2$
The girl is teasing the puppy.
(We use the subscripts 1 and 2 to indicate that the two noun phrases refer to different persons or things.)

*We will use the symbol NP from this point on to stand for noun phrase. VP stands for verb phrase.

62

Pattern 4: $NP_1 + VP_{tr} + NP_2 + NP_3$
    The man gave his daughter some money.
(We use the subscripts 1, 2, and 3 to indicate that the three noun phrases refer to different persons or things.)

Each of those sets of symbols represents the structure of thousands of sentences. For example, the set of symbols for Pattern 3, $NP_1 + VP_{tr} + NP_2$, can represent sentences like these:

The dog chewed this slipper.
A porpoise will find the shark.
Every boy will enjoy this dessert.
The skylark can see the insects.

The teacher may wish to draw a branching tree diagram like this on the chalkboard to show the structure of those sentences:

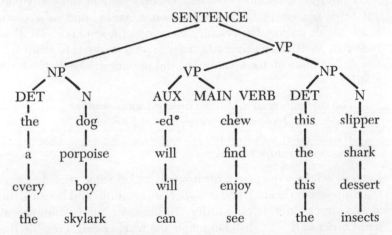

Branching-tree diagrams can serve as useful aids to the visually minded who need diagrams to help them understand sentence structure, but they are probably of little, if any, value as homework exercises. Research indicates that students profited little from having to diagram sentences in the traditional manner, and future research will probably indicate that students profit little from drawing branching-tree diagrams as homework.

*Although we do not want to labor the point, the auxiliary can consist of either the tense affix or a modal.

Review Exercise 1

To determine whether students understand the structures of the four basic sentence patterns, the teacher may give them these sets of symbols and ask students to write three basic sentences, i.e., sentences that contain only essential elements, for each set.

$$NP + VP_{intr}$$
$$NP_1 + VP_{li} + NP_1$$
$$NP + VP_{li} + Adj$$
$$NP_1 + VP_{tr} + NP_2$$
$$NP_1 + VP_{tr} + NP_2 + NP_3$$

FORM-WORD PHRASES

By carefully examining basic sentences, a student can easily pick out three classes of form words—nouns, verbs, and adjectives. Form words convey the primary meaning of a sentence. To illustrate that point, the teacher might ask several students to write sentences like these on the chalkboard and to underline only the form words:

The *carpenters* should have *ordered* some *lumber*.
Those *boys looked* very *weary*.
My *daughter* will *mail* the *packages*.
The *temperature* has been *rising*.

Each italicized sequence of form words makes some sense because the form words themselves carry specific meanings and because the words appear in a definite order. To illustrate the importance of word order in the English language, the teacher can scramble the form words in the above sequences to make groups of words like these:

lumber   ordered   carpenters
looked   boys   weary
packages   daughter   mail
rising   temperature

The only sequence that makes much sense is "rising temperature." The other three need to be rearranged or need more words added to the sequences to make sense.

Students should recall that form words can be easily detected because (a) they carry lexical meaning, (b) they fit into definite slots in basic sentences, (c) they pattern with certain structure words, and (d) they have endings. The endings and structure words form the framework of basic sentences. For example, if we remove the form words from the four sentences above and leave only the structure words and form-word endings, we have sentence frames like these:

1. The _____-s should have _____-ed some _____.
2. Those _____-s _____-ed very _____.
3. My _____ will _____ the _____-s.
4. The _____ has been _____-ing.

Alone, those structure words and endings carry little meaning, but they do provide the framework for an unlimited number of sentences. For example:

1. The stevedores should have loaded some cargo.
   The beatniks should have earned some money.
2. Those antiques looked very old.
   Those drinks tasted very bitter.
3. My ship will patrol the seas.
   My team will win the games.
4. The ship has been sailing.
   The horse has been running.

English has a very large number of form words—*Webster's Third New International Dictionary* defines more than 450,000—but it has only about two hundred structure words that are used over and over again to frame sentences. To help students see how they use those relatively few structure words with thousands of form words, the teacher may give exercises like these.

Review Exercise 2

For groups of words to be called phrases that can be put together to make grammatical sentences, the groups must consist of form words plus appropriate suffixes and structure words if necessary, and, of course, the groups must be put into meaningful sequences. To demonstrate those two aspects of grammatical structure, this exercise asks students to fill the blanks below with the proper form words and then to put the form-word phrases into appropriate sequences that make grammatical sentences.

	Structure Frames	Form Words
1.	is _____-ing	announcement
	the _____	make
	some _____-s	President
2.	may _____	pan
	quite _____	greasy
	those _____-s	become
3.	is going to _____	boss
	my _____	retire
4.	that _____	crime
	several _____-s	reporter
	have been _____-ing	investigate
5.	much too _____	test
	_____-ed	easy
	the last two _____-s	seem

Students should be able to explain why they selected a specific form word for each frame, and they should also be able to explain why they put the phrases into certain orders to make grammatical sentences.

Review Exercise 3

In the following sentences, some phrases are short and others are quite long and complicated. Each phrase contains only one form word. The student is asked (1) to underline each form word, excluding its suffix, (2) to indicate which class of form word it belongs to, and (3) to draw a line between the phrases.

              N   V   N

Example: Those *boys* / should have been *eat*ing / their *lunch*.

1. These three girls will wash all the clothes.
2. Very few students have completed that work.
3. Only that girl has been very good.
4. A thief must have taken all of the jewels.
5. Each of those dogs may have been chasing your cat.

Using the structure words and the suffixes of the form words in the sentences above, students should be able to build sentences of their own that have the same structures as those above but contain different form words.

Review Exercise 4

The following sentences, which are much like newspaper head-lines, have form words in appropriate sentence positions, but some of the sentences can be read with at least two different meanings because the structure frames are inadequate. The student is asked to rewrite each sentence three times, supplying more adequate structure frames. If the sentence is ambiguous, the student should clearly illustrate its two or more meanings.

Example: Harness falls.
That harness is falling.
Some of that harness fell.
Someone should harness those falls.

1. Waters flood valley.
2. Ship sails.
3. Women man lifeboats.
4. Judges pay.
5. School demands change.

THE STRUCTURE OF
FORM-WORD PHRASES

As we have already noted, structure frames of form-word phrases consist of both structure words and form-word suffixes. Frequently, structure words and form-word suffixes work together to form a sort of envelope into which a form word can be inserted. To help students see the structure of form-word phrases, the teacher may write phrases like these on the chalkboard:

those apples	some pipes
much blacker	somewhat larger
was returned	should have been following

Removing the form words without their suffixes, we have these structure frames:

those ＿＿＿-s   some ＿＿＿-s
much ＿＿＿-er   somewhat ＿＿＿-er
was ＿＿＿-ed   should have been ＿＿＿-ing

The structure frames for each class of form words are different from the frames for the other two classes. To illustrate that point, we can use a structure frame like this for nouns:

the ＿＿＿-s;
a structure frame like this for verbs:

is ＿＿＿-ing;
and a structure frame like this for adjectives:

much ＿＿＿-er.

Given those three structure frames, students should be able to put the following form words into their proper structure frames and tell which class the form word belongs to:

write   bureau   giraffe
short   magazine   build
inspect   grasp   poor
tight   clasp   strong

English is a fluid language. Instead of being able to use a word that we normally think of as a noun only in noun phrases, a speaker or writer can make that word function as a verb. For example, the word *chair* functions as a transitive verb and fits into a verb structure frame in a sentence like this:

The president *has* chair*ed* many meetings.

Of course, in a sentence like that, the word *chair* no longer refers to an object on which people sit but to the act of conducting a meeting. When words are moved from one class of form words to another, the meanings change.

Review Exercise 5

To show students how one word may function in two or three form classes, the teacher may give them an exercise like this one in which they try each of the words below in each of the structure frames and then list the possible form classes of the word in the blank after the word.

Structure frames: Noun—the ＿＿-s
Verb—is ＿＿-ing
Adjective—much ＿＿-er

1. walk ＿＿   5. sweet ＿＿   9. judge ＿＿
2. base ＿＿   6. train ＿＿   10. smart ＿＿
3. level ＿＿   7. love ＿＿   11. cut ＿＿
4. form ＿＿   8. fine ＿＿   12. brave ＿＿

Review Exercise 6

Students should name the form class of the italicized word in each sentence below and then rewrite the sentence, attempting to retain essentially the same meaning, by following the directions beneath the sentence.

Examples: a. John wrote a note with a *pen.*   N
Use *pen* as a verb.   *John penned a note.*
b. The sky became *dark.*   Adj
Use *dark* as a verb.   *The sky darkened.*

1. The cactus became covered with *blossoms.* ＿＿
   Use *blossom* as a verb. ＿＿＿＿＿＿＿＿＿＿＿＿
2. The airplane dropped *bombs* on the enemy. ＿＿
   Use *bomb* as a verb. ＿＿＿＿＿＿＿＿＿＿＿＿
3. My father finally gave his *consent.* ＿＿
   Use *consent* as a verb. ＿＿＿＿＿＿＿＿＿＿＿＿
4. Jim played a *trick* on me. ＿＿
   Use *trick* as a verb. ＿＿＿＿＿＿＿＿＿＿＿＿
5. Surely that policeman will give the old lady some *help.* ＿＿
   Use *help* as a verb. ＿＿＿＿＿＿＿＿＿＿＿＿

Students should decide which is the better sentence—the one given or their rewritten versions. They should be asked to defend their choices.

IRREGULAR NOUNS

Thus far we have used this structure frame, the ＿＿-s, for nouns. As students learned in grade seven, not all nouns form their

plurals, in writing, by adding the graphemes -*s* or -*es*. To review
irregular nouns, the teacher may write these nouns on the chalkboard and ask students to give the plural form of each:

mouse	child
tooth	man
goose	woman
sheep	ox
foot	deer
fish	basis
alumnus	criterion

After students have given the plural forms, the teacher may ask
questions like these: Which words form their plural by internal
vowel changes? Which words change endings? What are the endings? From what languages do the words come that form their
plurals, in writing, by adding endings other than -*s*?

To be uniform in our treatment of nouns in structure frames, we
shall always use the suffix -*s* to represent the plural forms. Thus,
the phrase, "the men," consists of the form word *man* plus the structure frame, "the ____-s."

IRREGULAR VERBS

Regular verbs have these four basic forms:

BASE FORM	THIRD PERSON PRESENT SINGULAR	PAST TENSE AND PAST PARTICIPLE	-*ing* FORM
walk	walks	walked	walking
talk	talks	talked	talking
perform	performs	performed	performing

Irregular verbs, with the exception of *be*, have these five forms:

BASE FORM	THIRD PERSON PRESENT SINGULAR	PAST TENSE	PAST PARTICIPLE	-*ing* FORM
go	goes	went	gone	going
run	runs	ran	run	running
sing	sings	sang	sung	singing

Review Exercise 7

To show the differences between regular and irregular verbs, the
teacher may give students an exercise like this in which they are

to supply the various forms of the following verbs and then answer the questions below:

BASE FORM	THIRD PERSON PRESENT SINGULAR	PAST TENSE	PAST PARTICIPLE	*-ing* FORM
decide				
help				
find				
speak				
shake				
tear				
turn				
drive				
sit				
choose				
run				
come				

Which verbs can be called *regular?* Why? Which verbs are *irregular?* Why? How are the past tense and the past participle of a regular verb formed? Of an irregular verb? Can you see any pattern among the irregular verbs?

ADJECTIVE PHRASES

Adjectives have these three forms:

sweet	sweeter	sweetest
pretty	prettier	prettiest

We call those forms the *positive, comparative,* and *superlative.* To form the comparative, in writing, we add the graphemes *-er* or we write the word *more* before the positive form. To form the superlative, we add the graphemes *-est* or we write the word *most* before the positive form.

The teacher may give students adjectives like these and ask them to supply the comparative and superlative forms:

beautiful	unstable	studious
ugly	dark	poor
clever	heavy	comfortable

What generalizations can students make after they have given the comparative and superlative forms of those adjectives? Which adjectives form their comparatives and superlatives by adding *-er* and *-est*? What do they have in common? Which adjectives form their comparatives and superlatives with the words *more* and *most*? What do they have in common? Can some adjectives form their comparatives and superlatives by adding *-er* and *-est* or by putting *more* and *most* in front of the positive forms? When do we use the positive form of adjectives? the comparative? the superlative?

These adjectives are irregular:

Positive	*Comparative*	*Superlative*
good	better	best
bad	worse	worst
little	less	least
much	more	most
many	more	most
well	better	best
ill	worse	worst
far	farther	farthest
far	further	furthest

Although we are now concerned primarily with the structure of phrases, we must pause briefly to observe in some detail the structure of certain form words. Each class of form words can be changed by adding affixes (an additional sound or group of sounds, or, in the case of writing, an additional grapheme or group of graphemes, which changes the meanings of the form words or which makes new form words). Knowledge of these affixes can be of value to students.

When we reviewed the structure affixes, we noted these graphemes:

for nouns: *-s, -'s, -s'*   (For all classes of words there
for verbs: *-s, -ed, -ing, -en*   are some irregular forms that
for adjectives: *-er, -est*   must be learned separately.)

In addition to these structure affixes, there are other affixes which we call derivational affixes. The following words are made up of base words plus derivational suffixes.

warmth	*warm* + *-th*
arrival	*arrive* + *-al*

dangerous	*danger* + *-ous*
creative	*create* + *-ive*
codify	*code* + *-ify*
capitalism	*capital* + *-ism*

Students should examine those words carefully. In each case, what class of form words does the word belong to *before* the derivational affix is attached? What is the class of the word *after* the affix is attached? Are there words in that list that do not change form-word classes when the derivational affix is attached?

The teacher may have students practice making derived words from the base words given below.

Base Word	Form-word →	Derived Word	Form-word
kind	*Adj*	*kindness*	noun
create	_____	_____	noun
solid	_____	_____	verb
care	_____	_____	adjective
involve	_____	_____	noun
believe	_____	_____	adjective
crystal	_____	_____	verb
friend	_____	_____	adjective

Most of the derivational affixes are suffixes, but these prefixes also occur with derived verbs:

be- + set (verb) = beset (verb)
en- + able (adjective) = enable (verb)
en- + throne (noun) = enthrone (verb)
em- + power (noun) = empower (verb)

There are also affixational changes that do not show in the written forms of words. Many words undergo a changing stress pattern as they move from one class to another. Examples:

STRESS ON THE FIRST SYLLABLE = NOUN	STRESS ON A SYLLABLE OTHER THAN THE FIRST = VERB
con' duct	con duct'
con' flict	con flict'
ex' tract	ex tract'
sub' ject	sub ject'
at' tribute	at trib' ute

It is possible to use more than one derivational affix on a base word, as the following examples show. The teacher may have students separate the base words and affixes as in the first example.

childishness	=	*child* + *-ish* + *-ness*
dramatization	=	_____
belittlement	=	_____
churlishness	=	_____
enactment	=	_____
shamefulness	=	_____

These are the common derivational affixes in English:

To form nouns:	-age, -al, -ant, ce, -er (-or), -ment, -tion, -ure, -ity, -ism, -dom, -ness, -hood, -y
To form verbs:	-ate, -en, -ify, -ize; (prefixes) en-, em-, be-
To form adjectives:	-able, -al, -ant (-ent), -ary, -ate, -ful, -ic, -ish, -ive, -less, -like, -ly, -ory, -ous, -some, -y

(To present these affixes to students inductively, the teacher should refer to the unit on prefixes and suffixes in *What Is Language?*, a volume in the English Curriculum Study Series.)

Review Exercise 8

Students are asked to put the base word, the form class, the derivational affixes, and the structure affixes under the appropriate column headings. Students should note that some words may have more than one derivational affix.

	BASE WORD—CLASS		DERIVATIONAL AFFIX —FORM CLASS		STRUCTURE AFFIX
Example:					
legalizes	legal	Adj	-ize	V	-s
1. favoritism					
2. foolishness					
3. neighborhoods					
4. departure					
5. momentary					
6. terrifying					

	BASE WORD—CLASS	DERIVATIONAL AFFIX —FORM CLASS	STRUCTURE AFFIX
7. verbalizes			
8. childlike			
9. artistic			
10. embodied			

EXPANDED NOUN PHRASES

Noun phrases are not always constructed of only a determiner plus a noun. All three form classes of words can enter a given noun phrase to provide more information about the head-noun.* For example:

John has dented *the car door.*
Frank put on *his blue jacket.*
Many cleaning fluids are inflammable.

The teacher might ask questions like these: What class does *car* belong to? What class does *blue* belong to? What class does *cleaning* belong to? School grammars have usually labeled all of these words "adjectives" when they entered noun phrases, reasoning that all of them "modify nouns." But clearly the words *car, blue,* and *cleaning* belong to three different classes of form words. They would appear in these typical structure phrases: the *cars,* much *heavier,* and is *cleaning.*

It is possible to insert several words into a noun phrase, like this:

three *dark oak slid*ing panels

What form classes do the inserted words belong to?

In the following phrases, students should label all words in each phrase, using the abbreviations *Det, N, V, Adj, Qual,* as in the example:

	Det	Qual	Adj	Adj	N
Example:	three	rather	ripe	purple	plums

1. several old vacuum cleaners
2. the wobbly ironing board
3. a rusty 1921 Model T Ford truck
4. some very old battered wooden barrels

---

*A head-noun is the principal noun in a noun phrase, and it is modified by other words.

Is any variation at all possible in the wording of the five phrases—
such as "purple rather ripe three plums" or "several vacuum old
cleaners"? From these few phrases, what generalizations can students make about the sequence of words in a noun phrase? (The
order normally is Det + Adj—or Qual + Adj— + Verbal + Noun
+ head-noun of the phrase.)

Noun phrases expand between the determiner and the head-
noun. Thus we might expand a phrase in stages, like this:

> the player
> the football player
> the college football player
> the participating college football player
> the oldest participating college football player*

The phrase builds up so that *football* expands upon *player, college*
expands upon *football player,* and so forth. The first words in the
phrase tend to modify all succeeding elements taken as a group.

Review Exercise 9

The student is asked to underline each noun phrase in the following sentences. Then, above each word in the noun phrase, he
is to write the appropriate label, using these abbreviations: *Det,
N, V, Adj, Qual.*

1. The two shrieking elementary school boys were arguing
   about the Russians' most recent space shot.
2. Those grimy service station attendants settled down into
   the immaculate brown leather furniture.
3. Several dozen reconditioned Dodge delivery trucks pulled
   out into the speeding freeway traffic.

The noun phrases in the following sentences contain some "of-
phrases." Observe how a complete noun phrase cometimes builds
up within another noun phrase.

---

*Of course nouns can also be modified by words following the noun phrase,
e.g., the oldest participating college football player there in the ball park.

4. One of the sharp-eyed detectives found these shredded strips of yellow silk material near the Van Dykes' private hunting lodge.
5. The tired government employee lay down on a thick layer of soft foam-rubber cushions.

Review Exercise 10

Whenever adjectives, nouns, and verbs are inserted into noun phrases, they make secondary statements about the head nouns in the phrases. Thus the phrase, "those streaking silver fighter planes," consists of the following separate statements which are inserted into the phrase, "those planes":

The planes *are streaking*. (verb phrase)
The planes are *silver*. (adjective phrase)
The planes are *fighters*. (noun phrase)

Students should rewrite each of the following noun phrases by inserting the additional statements into the phrase to make a natural-sounding noun phrase.

1. two blades _____
   The blades are dull.
   The blades have rusted.
   The blades are used on a saw.
2. the professor _____
   The professor is very intelligent.
   The professor is Chinese.
   The professor teaches biology.
3. a box of cards _____
   The box is large.
   The cards are sparkling.
   The cards are colorful.
   The cards are given at Christmas.
4. the streets _____
   The streets are in the city.
   The streets are slippery.
   The streets are slushy.
   The streets are filled with snow.

PROPER NOUNS AND
PERSONAL PRONOUNS

Many times a noun phrase will consist of simply the name of a person or place, like *John, Ethel, Mrs. Greene, Baltimore, Los Angeles, New South Wales,* and so forth. These names are called proper nouns.

A determiner normally does not occur with a proper noun. We say:

Ethel saw *John* in *Los Angeles.*

There are special cases, however, when it is possible to use determiners with proper nouns. Examples:

That Plymouth is located in Massachusetts, not in Indiana.
The two Elizabeths ruled England during periods of great change.
Only one of the Marys was in class today.

Determiners, then, are used with proper nouns when more than one thing bears the same name and the speaker or writer wants to single out one of the group or indicate that he means all or part of the things that bear the same name.

Often we wish to use a pronoun in place of a noun phrase. A pronoun is a word like *he, she, it, they,* and *them,* which can stand in place of a noun and carry the meaning of the noun it replaces. If we wish to replace the nouns in the sentences above, what pronouns would we use to fill the following blanks?

1. _____ saw _____ in Los Angeles.
2. _____ is located in Massachusetts, not in Indiana.
3. _____ ruled England during periods of great change.
4. Only one of _____ was in class today.

Pronouns are used in passages of connected material to avoid the repetition of phrases. In the following passage, students are asked to draw a circle around each pronoun, and then draw an arrow to the word that the pronoun stands for (the *antecedent* of the pronoun). The first pronoun is done as an example.

Today, police blamed the Irish Republican Army for the destruction of the Nelson monument. They said that the I.R.A. has shown signs of stepping up its activities recently.

Two girls, Brenda Moore and Angela Martin, had been standing near the statue just before it fell. Brenda said, "We had just walked away when we heard this terrible explosion behind us. It shook the whole street." She added that they were nearly struck by a falling stone.

Cab driver Stephen Maugham was waiting at a red light by the monument. Just as he got the green light he heard the explosion beside him. "I heard a sound like thunder," he said. "I just had time to get my fare and me out of there."

The Irish have complained about this statue for years. They have often voted to have it pulled down, but until now they have not attempted to destroy it.

Students should find a total of 21 words that they have learned to call pronouns. If they try to put the nouns back in place of the pronouns they will see how convenient—and necessary—pronouns are. Students should be asked these questions: Are determiners used with any of the pronouns in the above passage? Is it possible to have determiners with pronouns? Why are the "two girls" sometimes referred to as "we," but once referred to as "us"? Why is the cab driver sometimes "he" and sometimes "him"? Why is the cab driver sometimes "I" and sometimes "me"?

FUNCTIONS OF FORM-WORD PHRASES

At the beginning of this grammar study, we looked at four basic sentence patterns, and we observed that they were constructed of form-word phrases occurring in these sequences:

$NP + VP_{intr}$: intransitive-verb sentence

$NP_1 + VP_{li} + \left\{ \begin{array}{l} Adj \\ NP_1 \end{array} \right\}$: linking-verb sentence

$NP_1 + VP_{tr} + NP_2$: transitive-verb sentence
with direct object

$NP_1 + VP_{tr} + NP_2 + NP_3$: transitive-verb sentence with
indirect and direct objects

Since the seventh-grade course in grammar discusses in detail the functions of phrases in basic sentences, we shall merely add a few details as we review.

To review functions, we use the questions below to discuss these representative basic sentences:

1. The boy is sleeping.
2. The boy seems very lazy.
3. The boy became a scientist.
4. The boy has chopped some wood.

What is the subject of each sentence? How do you explain the subject function?

What is the predicate of each sentence? How do you explain the predicate function?

Which sentences contain three phrases? Which sentence contains only two phrases?

Which of the form words is always a part of the predicate?

If a sentence is formed of just two phrases, NP + VP, it contains an _____ verb. Why is the verb given this name?

Which phrase in these sentences is an adjective phrase? What is the function of the adjective phrase? What other phrases in these sentences have the same function?

The verbs *seems* and *became* are called _____ verbs. Why are these verbs given this name?

How do the functions of the two phrases "a scientist" and "some wood" differ? What is the name applied to the function of "some wood"? The verb "has chopped" is called a _____ verb. Why is the verb given this name?

Write the symbols that represent the form and function of the phrases in those four sentences.

The following brief discussion may serve as a guide to the conclusions students reached during their examination of functions in basic sentences.

Sentences are divided by function into two parts, the subject and the predicate. The subject of the sentence names that which the sentence is talking about, and the predicate makes a statement about the subject. (See page ooo of grade seven for a more complete definition.) In basic sentences we always place the subject first in the sentence. We shall use the subscript s to identify the subject function in labeling phrases, like this: NP_s.

In the predicate, it is the verb which determines the pattern of the sentence. If the verb is *intransitive,* as in the sentence "The boy is sleeping," the basic sentence contains only two phrases, and the sentence pattern can be written in a set of symbols like this:

$$NP_s + VP_{intr}$$

We call this *basic-sentence pattern one.* In this pattern, the subject contains one phrase, and the predicate contains one phrase.

If a *linking* verb occurs, as in Pattern 2, the sentence must have a third position following the verb, and the third position must give more information about the subject. The phrase in the third position is called the *subject complement* (sc). This subject complement can be either a noun phrase or an adjective phrase:

The boy seems *very lazy.* ($NP_s + VP_{li} + Adj_{sc}$)
The boy became *a scientist.* ($NP_s + VP_{li} + NP_{sc}$)

We may represent the linking-verb sentence, *basic-sentence pattern two,* in this way:

$$NP_s + VP_{li} + \begin{Bmatrix} NP_{sc} \\ Adj_{sc} \end{Bmatrix}$$

The braces mean that one, and only one, of the enclosed phrases is to be used. Common linking verbs are *seem, become, appear, feel, taste, sound, look,* and forms of *be.* As their name suggests, they serve to "link" the subject phrase to the subject-complement phrase. In this sentence pattern, the predicate is formed of the verb phrase plus the subject complement.

If a *transitive* verb occurs, as in the sentence "The boy has chopped some wood," the sentence must again have a third position, but this time the third position is occupied by the *object,* which is always a noun phrase. Except for those special cases in which a reflexive pronoun is used (as in "John cut *himself*"), the object phrase has a different referent from that of the subject phrase. In our symbolic statement of this sentence pattern, *basic-sentence pattern three,* we use the subscript *o* to represent the object function.

$$NP_s + VP_{tr} + NP_o$$

In this pattern, the predicate consists of the verb phrase plus the object.

Review Exercise 11

For each of the following sentences, students are asked to (a) draw a vertical line between the subject and predicate and to (b) write the symbols which represent the basic-sentence pattern.

Example: The three ladies / look very weary.
$$NP_s + VP_{li} + Adj_{sc}$$

1. Most of the leaves have fallen.
2. That boy may have found your wallet.
3. John seems quite dependable.
4. Two cowboys were driving that herd of cattle.
5. Captain Fitzhugh must have resigned.
6. Several of the ships sank.
7. Professor Knox has become a realtor.
8. That gang of robbers may have derailed the train.

VARIATIONS OF THE
BASIC SENTENCE PATTERNS

The verbs *be* and *have* are the most common verbs in English. They occur as auxiliaries in many of the sentences we construct, and they also occur very frequently as main verbs. They are of special interest—and present special problems.

The following sentences have forms of the verb *be* as the main verb:

Sam is quite tall.
I am ready.
All of the students are at their desks.
Susie was one of the cheerleaders.
Three of the senators were members of a special commission.
Tom has been down the river in a canoe.
"Very" is a qualifier.
Sam was being difficult.
Over the fence should be out.

Students should be asked questions like these: What are the different forms of *be*? What are the three present-tense forms? What are the two past-tense forms? What is the past participle form? In what ways are the forms of *be* different from the forms of other verbs? What sentence structures are peculiar to the verb *be*—that would not be possible with verbs like *seem, become, appear,* and so forth? What is unusual about the sentence "Over the fence should be out"? Which sentence pattern does the verb *be* belong to?

Students may make the following generalizations:

The verb *be* is the most common linking verb and may be considered as a constituent of the pattern-two sentence. It is unique, however, in being the only true *equational* verb. We can use other linking verbs to say "John *appears (seems,* or *becomes)* tired, but we can use only the verb *be* to say "John *is* tired." *Be* can be used to equate all kinds of things, such as:

> Over the fence should be out.
> Right is wrong.
> "Very" is a qualifier.
> *?* is a question mark.

Also, *be* is the only verb that has more than five forms in its conjugation. An irregular verb like *sing* has these five forms:

> present—sing   past participle—sung
>   sings
> past—sang   present participle—singing

But *be* has eight forms:

> infinitive—be   past—was
> present—am   were
>   are   past participle—been
>   is   present participle—being

Be is very often followed by a prepositional phrase, or phrases, rather than by an adjective phrase or noun phrase, as other linking verbs are. For example:

> All of the students are *at their desks.*
> Tom has been *down the river in a canoe.*

In spite of all these special characteristics, *be* may, for the sake of simplicity, be considered one of the linking verbs.

The verb *have* is a transitive verb, for it occurs in a pattern which has a noun phrase functioning as an object in the third position. It differs from the vast majority of transitive verbs in one way; it can seldom be used in the passive. With most transitive verbs, we have two forms like these:

Active: John found those shoes.
Passive: Those shoes were found by John.

But with *have,* these two forms do not occur:

Active: John had those shoes.
Passive: Those shoes were had by John. (ungrammatical)

There are very few other verbs like *have* that do not have the passive form, but we need not be concerned about them as a separate class of verbs.

There are many transitive-verb sentences in English which require a second complement in addition to the noun phrase that functions as an object. We shall look at just a few of them.

The most common of these sentence types is the *indirect-object* sentence. For example:

John gave the teacher his paper.

The indirect-object sentence, which we shall call *basic-sentence pattern four,* may be expressed symbolically like this:

$NP_s + VP_{tr} + NP_{io} + N_o$
John   gave   the teacher   his paper.

In that sentence pattern the indirect object *precedes* the object, and the object occurs in the fourth sentence position. Sentences which follow pattern four may be rewritten in the following alternate form:

$$NP_s + VP_{tr} + NP_o + \begin{Bmatrix} to \\ for \end{Bmatrix} + NP_{io}$$

For example:

John gave *the teacher* his paper. (or) John gave his paper *to the teacher.*
John bought *his father* a pen. (or) John bought a pen *for his father.*

The other sentences which have four sentence positions are not considered major sentence patterns in this program. We include them here only as examples of sentences containing four major phrase positions. In all of these sentences the second complement *follows* the object.

The object-complement sentence:

$$NP_s + VP_{tr} + NP_o + \begin{cases} NP_{oc} \\ Adj_{oc} \end{cases}$$

The coach   made   Dick   *his assistant.*

(The noun phrases in positions three and four have the same referent.)

Sentences requiring verbal complements:

$NP_s + VP_{tr} + NP_o +$ participle
Henry   caught   the boys   *stealing his apples.*
(participle phrase)

$NP_s + VP_{tr} + NP_o +$ infinitive
Jim   urged   his friends   *to vote for him.* (infinitive phrase)

Exercise

Students should write the symbolic statement of each of the sentences below according to the example.

Example: John forced the little boy to carry his books.
$$NP_s + VP_{tr} + NP_o + \text{infinitive}$$

1. Mr. Jones has had his problems.
2. Horace should have been driving his own car.
3. The teacher found some of us carving the desk tops.
4. Mr. Marx was under the truck.
5. Sergeant O'Neil gave the boys a lecture.
6. Mrs. Jadis asked the attendant to vacuum-clean her car.
7. The Smiths will be having some visitors.
8. Susan should have been an interior decorator.
9. Fred may have bought his girl friend a box of chocolates.
10. The committee has appointed Hector its temporary chairman.

PREPOSITIONAL PHRASES

Thus far the only grammatical structures we have examined in detail are form-word phrases and the basic sentence patterns that can be produced by stringing those phrases together. Now we are

ready to have students consider sentences like these, in which the
second noun phrase is connected to the rest of the sentence by the
italicized preposition.

John walked *into* the building.
John walked *around* the building.
John walked *between* the buildings.
John walked *out of* the building.
John drove *under* the bridge.
John drove *over* the bridge.
John drove *across* the bridge.
John stood *near* the tree.
John stood *behind* the tree.
John stood *in front of* the tree.
John stood *beside* the tree.

A preposition is nearly always followed by a noun phrase in a
structure that is called a *prepositional phrase* (pp). The noun in the
prepositional phrase functions as the *object of the preposition* (op).

Exercise

Students are asked to write the symbolic representations of the
form and function of the form-word phrases and of the noun in the
prepositional phrase in the sentences below.

Example: John found my shoe under his chair.
$$NP_s + VP_{tr} + NP_o + prep + NP_{op}$$

1. Harvey threw a pass into the end zone.
2. Those buses go by the post office.
3. Kenneth was a sergeant in the Marine Corps.
4. Those prisoners have dug a tunnel underneath the road.
5. Two MP's stopped all the cars at the gate.
6. Joe should have put his watch on the desk.
7. Most of the delegates stayed in a motel.
8. The pilot flew along the coast.
9. Dad keeps his rifle above the fireplace.
10. The lawyers continued their argument in my office.

PLACEMENT OF
PREPOSITIONAL PHRASES

Prepositional phrases often occur at the end of sentences, but they can also come at the beginning or in the middle of sentences, as the following italicized prepositional phrases show:

> Miss Ames kept Eddie in her classroom *during recess.*
> *During recess,* Miss Ames kept Eddic in her classroom.
> The history teacher *in our school* is always cheerful.

(The comma following the prepositional phrase, *during recess,* in the second sentence above is not mandatory, but writers frequently use a comma after introductory phrases, and speakers frequently pause briefly after such phrases.)

Not all prepositional phrases are as movable as *during recess* in the first two sentences above. For example, few of us would say or write this sentence:

> *In her classroom,* Miss Ames kept Eddie during recess.

Exercise

To give students practice in working with prepositional phrases, the teacher may have them rewrite the following sentences, moving a prepositional phrase or two to the beginning of the sentences whenever possible.

1. The herd of elk wandered through the mountains in search of food for months.
2. Tom has been leaving his lunch pail on the table in his boss's office since last October.
3. Sue pushed a note into Jim's room at midnight through a crack in the wall.
4. Mr. Jones stood beside Frank throughout the trial because of his confidence in his friend.
5. The race at the Speedway will start by eleven o'clock in spite of the rain.
6. Harold hung the key on a hook in the closet beneath the stairway for your convenience.

ADVERBIAL AND
ADJECTIVAL PHRASES

Prepositional phrases function most frequently either as adverbials or adjectivals. For example, in the sentences below, the first prepositional phrase functions as an adjectival, telling *which* keys, and the second functions as an adverbial, telling *where* they were found.

The custodian found the keys *to your car* in the wastebasket.

An adverbial prepositional phrase usually occurs at the end of a sentence as an optional element, but, as we have seen, it can also occur at the beginning of a sentence. The function of an adverbial phrase is usually expressed through a *some* element. For prepositional phrases, the *some* elements are usually expressed as *somewhere* and *sometime*.

Adjectival prepositional phrases enter a sentence as a sub-part of the noun phrase. In the example below, "to your car" is a sub-part of the noun phrase, "the keys," as this diagram illustrates:

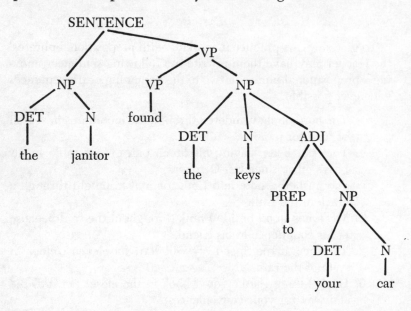

Thus a prepositional phrase used as an adjectival *immediately follows* the noun which it modifies, and it is not movable, as an adverbial phrase is.

ADVERBIALS

We start this brief review of adverbials by suggesting that the teacher write five sentences like these on the chalkboard and ask several students to volunteer to underline the parts of the sentences that would *not* be included in the basic sentence patterns. The student volunteers should also draw diagonal lines between the form-word phrases, and then indicate, by symbols, the form and function of each phrase that is a part of the basic sentence pattern.

Example: Farmer Jones / found / a fox / *in the chicken coop.*
$NP_s + VP_{tr} + NP_o$

1. One of the grooms gave the horse a good workout yesterday.
2. Tom was enthusiastic about football during the summer.
3. This elevator is going down.
4. Sally filed those letters in the top drawer.
5. The boy in the first row becomes a spelunker every Saturday.

We can help students recall information about adverbial phrases by asking questions like these:

1. Where in the above sentences do the adverbial elements appear? (At the end of the sentences.)
2. What kinds of information do the adverbials provide? (Sentences 1, 2, and 5—time; sentences 3 and 4—direction and place.)
3. In the seventh grade, we used *some* elements to represent functions. What *some* elements would you use to identify the function of the adverbials in the above sentences? (Sentences 1, 2, and 5—*sometime;* sentences 3 and 4—*somewhere.*)
4. Which of those adverbials can be moved to other positions in the sentences? (These changes can be made:

Yesterday one of the grooms gave the horse a good workout.
During the summer Tom was enthusiastic about football.
Every Saturday the boy in the first row becomes a spelunker.

Other changes would not be made by native speakers of English.)

5. What is the function of the movable adverbials? *(Sometime.)* The teacher may wish to have students examine other sentences containing adverbials to discover whether the *sometime* adverbial seems to be more movable than other adverbials.
6. What is the component part of each of those adverbials? (Sentence 1—noun phrase; sentence 2—prepositional phrase; sentence 3—adverb; sentence 4—prepositional phrase; sentence 5—noun phrase.)

ADVERBIAL FUNCTIONS

Each of the following basic sentences contains at least two adverbials. The student is to draw vertical lines between the form-word phrases which form the basic sentence. Then he should draw a circle around each of the adverbials. Finally, he should write the questions he would usually ask if he wished to learn the information contained in each of the adverbials.

Example: Farmer Jones / found / a fox /(in the chicken coop)
(last night.)
Where did Farmer Jones find a fox last night?
When did Farmer Jones find a fox in the chicken coop?

1. Pete will be going home after the game.
2. That kind of airplane can go around the world once a day.
3. The team has been playing very aggressively all season.
4. Jim went to the mountains because of the recent snowstorm.
5. Carol practices the piano for two hours every Saturday.
6. Mike has to walk two miles to school every day.

Though adverbial functions are generally expressed as *sometime, somewhere,* and *somehow,* there are time and place relationships that must be more explicitly stated. For example, in sentence 3 above, we would be more accurate if we stated the function of *all season* as *some duration of time* rather than just *sometime.* This more precise statement of function is indicated by the question we would usually ask: not "*When* has the team been playing very aggressively?" but "*How long* has the team been playing very aggressively?"

Other adverbials in those sentences have functions other than *sometime, somewhere,* and *somehow.* We would state their functions like this:

> Sentence 2: "around the world"—some distance
> "once a day"—some frequency
> Sentence 4: "because of the recent snowstorm"—some reason
> Sentence 5: "for two hours"—some duration of time
> "every Saturday"—some frequency
> (though *sometime* is correct, too)
> Sentence 6: "two miles"—some distance
> "every day"—some frequency

GENERAL ADVERBIALS

The teacher might ask students the function of each of the following italicized adverbials:

1. The ships left the harbor *then.* (sometime)
2. Visitors may go *there* on Tuesdays. (somewhere)
3. The posse rode off *that way.* (either some direction or some manner—"The posse rode off *toward the mountains,*" or "The posse rode off *angrily.*")
4. No man can stay under water *that long.* (some duration of time)

While we can state the functions of those adverbials, we cannot get much *meaning* out of them. *Then* does not really tell us when the ships left the harbor, and *there* does not tell us where visitors may go on Tuesdays. Thus, this kind of adverbial, which we shall call a "general" adverbial, is actually a *replacement* for another adverbial, much as a pronoun is a replacement for a noun. Adverbials like *then* and *there* have meaning only as they refer back to details previously mentioned. For example:

> Dad and I were in Chicago last week. We picked out my bicycle *then.*

Exercise 1

The student should write the form and function of each of the italicized adverbials.

1. The boys run *across the street everyday*.
2. Mrs. Adams sat *under the drier patiently for several hours*.
3. We are going *there next year*.
4. The fire truck dashed *through the streets toward the fire*.
5. The farmer *often* plows his field *that way*.

Exercise 2

The student should rewrite the following sentences, placing the adverbials in alternate positions.

1. Sally earned all A's without any effort in the first grade.
2. The hunters arrived at the lodge one by one late in the afternoon.
3. The screams of the multitude echoed again and again through the streets of Paris.
4. Cars raced down the highway all night long.
5. The sheriff fired one shot into the air as a warning.

Exercise 3

The student may simplify the statement of adverbials by using the general function label *adv* rather than by giving the more specific *some* element.

Example: Yesterday John found a crayfish in his shoe.
$$N_{adv} + NP_s + VP_{tr} + NP_o + PP_{adv}$$

The student should write the form and function symbols for all the phrases in the following sentences.

1. Tomorrow the team will be traveling to Boston.
2. None of our teachers gives tests the last day before vacation.
3. Those boys went home before three o'clock.
4. Don had been quietly sunning himself there for several hours.
5. At midnight Mr. Parsons turned the clock back one hour.

ADVERBIALS IN VERB PHRASES

We frequently use adverbials like these in verb phrases:

not	always
never	usually
seldom	only
hardly	even
frequently	often

In the sentences below, we can see how some of those adverbials fit into verb phrases:

1. John was on time.
   John was not on time.
   John was never on time.
   John was always on time.
   John was usually on time.
2. John was studying.
   John was not studying.
   John was always studying.
   John was hardly studying.
   John was only studying.
3. John could have been studying.
   John could not have been studying.
   John could hardly have been studying.

By carefully examining those sentences, students should note that the adverbials follow a form of the verb *be* when it is the main verb in a sentence and that they follow the first auxiliary in a verb phrase.

In sentences containing intransitive verbs, the placement of some adverbials depends upon the writer, i.e., it is a matter of rhetoric, not of grammar, as in:

John frequently studies. John often studies.
John studies frequently. John studies often.

But most native speakers would say

John never studies. John hardly studies.

and not

John studies never. John studies hardly.

In sentences containing transitive verbs, the placement of some adverbials also depends upon the writer or speaker, as in:

John frequently studies algebra.
John studies algebra frequently.

But most native speakers would say

John never studies algebra.

and not

John studies algebra never.

When native speakers and writers use *not* with any one-word verb except a form of *be,* they insert a form of the verb *do* into the verb phrase, as in:

John does not study.
John does not study algebra.
John does not seem tired.

A native speaker would not say

John not studies.   John not studies algebra.

Exercise

The student should rewrite each of the following sentences by inserting some or all of the adverbials listed in parentheses. For some sentences the student can write several different sentences.

Example: The herd of elk wandered. (not, into the fields, for months)
For months the herd of elk did not wander into the fields.

1. The jailer slid a cup of stew. (always, through the small opening, at noon)
2. Mr. Jones forgot his friend. (not, for a moment, throughout the trial)
3. The races start. (hardly, ever, at three o'clock, promptly, at the Speedway)
4. Ned was at home. (not, always, probably, after eight o'clock)

5. Carolyn likes school. (not, always, only in July, early in the morning)
6. Sharon goes swimming. (never, usually, at midnight, in the river)

SIMPLE TRANSFORMATIONS

The sentences below represent the four basic sentence patterns, though their structures may be somewhat obscured by the adverbials. To show students the basic sentence structures, the teacher may have volunteers underline the phrases that make up the basic sentences and label them NP or VP, as has been done in the first sentence with italics.

    NP   VP
1. At dawn *the three spies* *waited* anxiously by their radio.
2. Certainly Mr. Kennedy could not have been our president in 1958.
3. This morning a lifeguard courageously saved that child from the surf.
4. Last week during the banquet at the school cafeteria, the coach proudly gave members of the team their letters.

We have these basic sentences:

1. The three spies waited.
2. Mr. Kennedy could have been our president.
3. A lifeguard saved that child.
4. The coach gave members of the team their letters.

We have already observed that adverbials are movable phrases which can be placed in various positions in sentences largely at the writer's option. We have not, however, experimented with moving the basic-sentence phrases into different sentence positions. Using the four basic sentences above, we can see how much flexibility of structure is possible in basic sentences.

In basic sentence one, which contains only two phrases, the only possible rewriting is " Waited the three spies," which is not an acceptable structure unless we retain the adverbial of place and write this sentence: "By their radio waited the three spies."

Can students say, "At dawn waited the three spies"? As they try the various combinations of phrases, what generalizations can they make? (Inversion of the two phrases is sometimes possible when an adverbial appears in position one, but it is not possible otherwise.) These are examples of pattern-one sentences with adverbials in position one:

1. *In the field* lay two of the wrecks.
2. *On Monday* appeared a strange sight.
3. *Suddenly* arose a great storm.

Sentences 2 and 3 are artificial inversions which native speakers would probably not say. They seem to be more acceptable in "poetic" passages than in most prose contexts, e.g., "At dawn nods the dew-pearl'd rose."

In basic sentence two there are three phrases with these possible arrangements:

1. Could have been Mr. Kennedy our president.
2. Mr. Kennedy our president could have been.
3. Our president could have been Mr. Kennedy.
4. Could have been our president Mr. Kennedy.
5. Our president Mr. Kennedy could have been.

Only 3 makes a good sentence because the two noun phrases refer to the same person. Therefore, the only flexibility of structure in pattern-two sentences is the reversal of the two noun phrases.

If, in pattern two, an adjective phrase had been in position three, rearrangements would not have been possible. For example, if the sentence had read: "Certainly Mr. Kennedy could not have been *very sick* in 1958," there would be no acceptable rearrangements of the phrases with the exception of the movable prepositional phrase, *in 1958*.

In basic sentence three, we could have these rearrangements of phrases:

1. A lifeguard that child saved.
2. Saved that child a lifeguard.
3. Saved a lifeguard that child.
4. That child a lifeguard saved.
5. That child saved a lifeguard.

None of those rearrangements preserves the original meaning of the sentence.

In basic sentence four, there are twelve possible rearrangements of phrases, none of which is acceptable.

Thus we can see that stable basic-sentence structure is essential to sentence meaning. The reader or listener expects phrases to fall into certain patterns, and if his expectations are not fulfilled, he will be confused—at least until other clues in the sentence or his own logic provides the probable intended meaning.

There are, however, some standard variations in sentence patterns that are essential to the writing of certain kinds of sentences. These variations are called sentence *transformations*. We will look at a variety of these transformations in the remainder of our study of grammar. In the seventh-grade grammar unit, we examined in some detail the transformations of basic sentences called the *simple transformations*, so we shall briefly review them now, adding a few details as we proceed.

QUESTION TRANSFORMATIONS

We start with this basic sentence:

John has signed the check.

If we want to know whether or not John has signed the check, we ask this question: "Has John signed the check?" This is called a *yes-no question* because a question in this form is requesting a *yes* or *no* answer.

If we want to know *why* John has signed the check, we would ask "Why has John signed the check?" We do not expect a "yes" or "no" answer, but we do expect some explanation for John's action. This type of question is called a *wh-question* because the question is always introduced with a *wh-word*—one of the question-asking words like *when, where, why, what*, and *how, how long*, and so forth.

To show students what changes we make in the basic sentence to form each of those questions, we can have them compare these statement and question forms of the same sentence:

1. Yes-no question transformation:
   John has signed the check.   Has John signed the check?
   (auxiliary placed ahead of the subject to form the question)

2. Wh-question transformation:
John has signed the check. Why has John signed the check?
(wh-word + yes-no question transform)

Exercise

For each of the following sentences the student should: (1) Draw a circle around the first auxiliary word in the verb phrase; then, beneath the example sentence, he should write a yes-no question by placing the encircled auxiliary word ahead of the subject noun-phrase. (2) Compose the wh-question which he would ask to learn the information italicized in each sentence.

Example: The waves (have) been pounding the sea wall *all day*.
Have the waves been pounding the sea wall all day?
How long have the waves been pounding the sea wall?

1. Jim has been catching *at least ten fish* every day.
2. The wind has blown *all those leaves* into Mr. Jordan's yard.
3. *The groundskeeper* should have spread lawn food on the fairways.
4. Mr. Michaels may stay *at our house* during his visit.
5. You should not stand up in a canoe *at any time*.

(Note how the contraction "shouldn't" seems more natural in the question forms.)

MORE ON QUESTIONS

As long as the verb phrase contains at least one auxiliary word, the questions are always formed the same way. But a somewhat different transformational process is involved when there is no auxiliary word in the verb phrase. For example:

John signed the check.   (becomes)   Did John sign the check?

In that question we have introduced a verb *do* into the verb phrase. The question transform is always produced by putting the auxiliary first in the sentence. If there is no auxiliary, one must be introduced. Thus, the verb *do* is used.

The student should compare the statement and question forms of this transformation:

John signed the check.   Did John sign the check?

The *-ed* is dropped from *signed;* the past tense of *do* is introduced and is put into the position ahead of the subject. If we examine that transformation closely, we see that essentially the same process is involved as in the case of the verb phrase which contains an auxiliary word. The auxiliary affix by itself can be the entire auxiliary of the verb phrase and can function in the same way as the auxiliary word. If we treat the auxiliary affix as if it were an auxiliary word, the same change takes place in both question transformations.

John *has signed* the check.   *Has* John *signed* the check?
John *sign + -ed* the check.   *-ed* John sign the check?

But, of course, the *-ed* affix cannot stand by itself, so we introduce the *do* to carry the affix.

Did John *sign* the check? (The past tense of *do*—do + -ed— is *did*.)

We have already observed that *do* enters a verb phrase to help form a negative when there is no auxiliary word, as in:

John *did not* sign the check.

That, of course, is the same principle that applies in the question transformation. Since "John -ed not sign the check" is impossible, *do* is introduced to carry the past-tense affix.

Exercise

The student should write the yes-no and wh-question transforms and make other alterations in the sentences as requested in the instructions following each example sentence. We have used *some* elements to indicate which wh-questions should be used.

Example: Dr. Watson found Sherlock Holmes at Baker Street
for-some-reason.
Yes-no question: Did Dr. Watson find Sherlock Holmes at
Baker Street?

Yes-no question + not: Didn't Dr. Watson find Sherlock
Holmes at Baker Street?

Wh-question + not: Why didn't Dr. Watson find Sherlock
Holmes at Baker Street?

1. The police have been searching for clues *someplace* since
Tuesday night.

   Yes-no question:
   Wh-question:

2. The explorers discovered a new civilization *somehow*.
   Yes-no question:
   Wh-question:
   Yes-no question + not:

3. *Some* countries used slaves for cheap labor.
   Yes-no question:
   Yes-no question + not:
   Wh-question + not + ever:

4. The profession of politics should be highly respected *for
some reason*.

   Yes-no question:
   Yes-no question + not + always:
   Wh-question + not + always:

THERE-EXPLETIVE
TRANSFORMATION

Many times writers and speakers wish to interchange the phrases
within basic sentences, but, as we learned earlier, interchanging
phrases usually destroys the structure of the sentence. However,
there are transformational processes which permit certain rearrangements. One of these is the *there*-expletive transformation.

Using *there* as the introductory word in each sentence, we can
rewrite these sentences:

1. A train is loading at gate 16.
   There is a train loading at gate 16.
2. A few apples are in the barrcl.
   There are a few apples in the barrel.
3. Some time was left after the test.
   There was some time left after the test.

4. A hermit had been living in the cave.
   There had been a hermit living in the cave.

Students should examine the two forms of each sentence.

What is common to all the verbs in those sentences? (*Be* is either a main verb or an auxiliary.)

What does *there* contribute to the sentence? (Fills the space vacated by the subject. *There* is called an *expletive*.)

What change takes place in the basic sentence during this transformation? (*There* comes first, replacing the subject. The subject follows the verb *be*. Thus, this structure is formed: There + a form of the verb *be* + subject + remainder of the sentence.)

Look carefully at the determiner in each subject noun phrase. What feature is common to these determiners? (They are all indefinite determiners.)

Each student should make up some basic sentences of his own and write *there* transformations using the form below as a guide. Is he able to find some sentences which can be transformed in this way even though they do not contain the verb *be*? Are there sentences containing *be* which cannot be transformed in this way? Is it necessary to have an indefinite determiner in the subject noun phrase?

This sentence has been done as an example: "Some monkeys were swinging through the trees."

There	Form of *be*	Subject	Remainder
There	were	some monkeys	swinging through the trees

Though the *there* transformation is usually an optional rewriting, some sentences sound strange unless they are transformed. For example:

1. There are three winners in every game.   Three winners are in every game.
2. There were not many dangers along the river.   Many dangers were not along the river.   Not many dangers were along the river.
3. Then there was a riot.   Then a riot was.   A riot was then.   Then was a riot.

4. There shouldn't have been more than one answer. More than one answer shouldn't have been. No more than one answer should have been.

Students should note that in all of those sentences the main verb is a form of *be*.

Many times, the remainder of the sentence, as given in the form above, can be substituted for *there* to produce a sentence like "Swinging through the trees were some monkeys." (How many of the sentences students wrote could be rearranged that way?)

Thus we see that there can be flexibility of structure in a basic sentence if certain rules are followed. One of the rules is that the subject phrase may occur after *be* (as verb or as auxiliary) if *there* is inserted into the position previously occupied by the subject. We may write this general rule in symbolic form like this:

$$\text{NP}_s + be + \text{remainder} \Rightarrow \text{There} + be + \text{NP}_s + \text{remainder}$$

That is only a very rough statement of the transformation, however. There are many sentences which cannot be transformed even though they seem to fit into that general pattern, and some sentences may accept the *there* transformation even though the verb *be* does not occur, e.g., "There *exist* many other translations of the text."

Exercise

The student should write *there*-expletive transforms of each of the following sentences.

1. Huge waves had been lashing the shore all week long.
2. Many wars have been waged since 1776.
3. Three storm centers were developing in the Gulf.
4. No ladies should have been in the audience.
5. Why haven't any of your classmates been selected?

THE PASSIVE TRANSFORMATION

A second method of interchanging the phrases of basic sentences is the *passive transformation*. Whereas the *there* transformation is limited to certain changes when *be* occurs in the verb phrase, the passive transformation is limited to pattern three, transitive-verb sentences.

Any native speaker of English can perform the passive transformation automatically, as students will learn by rearranging the phrases in these three sentences by making the italicized phrases the subjects.

>   Example: The Blue Devils defeated *our team.*
>   Our team was defeated by the Blue Devils.

1. The police follow *suspicious strangers.*
2. Those boys may not have taken *your bicycle.*
3. The excavators are beginning *the work.*

We can help students understand the operations they have performed by asking questions like these:

1. How many form-word phrases are in each of those sentences? (Three)
2. When the underlined phrase—in position three—moves to position one, what happens to the phrase that was originally in position one? (Moves to position three, after the word *by.*)
3. What changes are made in the verb? (A form of *be* is introduced. The main verb becomes the past participle form. Note the forms *taken* and *begun.*)
4. In sentence 2, at what point does the auxiliary *be* enter the verb phrase? (After *have*—at the end of the auxiliary)
5. Why are there *two* forms of *be* in sentence 3 after the transformation—"The work *is being* begun by the excavators."? (There is a form of *be* in the basic sentence; when *be* is added to make the transformation, there are then two forms of *be* in the sentence.)
6. In sentence 3, why is the auxiliary *are* in the basic sentence changed to *is* in the transform? (*The excavators,* a plural noun, is subject of the basic sentence; *the work,* a singular noun, is subject of the transform. The verb must agree in number with its subject.)

If we examine a large number of passive transformations, we shall find that these facts which we have observed above are generally true of this transformation: (a) the two noun phrases change position; (b) a form of *be* enters the verb phrase at the end of the auxiliary; (c) the main verb occurs in the past participle form; (d) the structure word *by* precedes the final noun phrase. We may express these facts in a relatively simple symbolic statement (let NP_1 stand for the subject phrase in the basic sentence, and NP_2 stand for the object phrase):

$$NP_1 + Aux + VP_{tr} + NP_2 \Rightarrow NP_2 + Aux + be + VP_{tr}\text{-en} + by + NP_1$$

Students should make up several pattern-three basic sentences of their own. They should write passive transforms by filling in a form like the one below. This sentence has been done as an example: "A plumber can repair that faucet."

NP_2	Aux	be	VP_{tr}-en	by	NP_1
that faucet	can	be	repaired	by	a plumber

In general, the passive-voice transformation is a synonymous rewriting of the original sentence; we have simply inverted the whole structure. It is called *passive* because the subject of the sentence is no longer the "doer" of the action in the sentence, but the "receiver." To illustrate:

Basic sentence—Sally kissed Egbert.
Passive transform—Egbert was kissed by Sally.

Egbert is the *object* in the basic sentence, and, logically, he is still the *object* in the transform. In the transform, the verb *was kissed* states the action which is performed on the *passive* subject, Egbert. The basic sentence, before being transformed, is called *active*, in contrast to the *passive* transform.

Though the passive is a synonymous rewriting, there are some differences in emphasis between the two sentences. In the passive, the emphasis is placed on *Sally*. The unusual placement of the doer of the action (Sally) at the end of the sentence, rather than in the subject position, focuses attention on her.

Usually, the active sentence is preferable to the passive, unless the writer wishes to place some special emphasis on certain phrases, as suggested above. The active sentence uses fewer words and conforms better to basic English structure. Also, the passive, unless carefully used, can become a very clumsy construction.

All of the sentences we have examined so far are composed of only three form-word phrases that make up the basic sentence. Usually, such sentences are not informative enough, because normally we want to give additional information through adverbials, adjectives, and so forth. Thus the sentences below might be more representative of real sentences. Can students make them passive?

1. Last night scientists at Cape Kennedy launched a new satellite into orbit.
2. Max probably should have bought a new set of golf clubs long ago.
3. The delivery man had to carry all five cartons of books up two flights of stairs.

If students can make those passive transforms, they should be able to solve these somewhat more complicated problems:

1. Transform the following sentence into its passive form:

> The garage attendant did not wash the windows on my car. (The windows on my car were not washed by the garage attendant.)

Look at the verbs of the basic sentence and the transform. How do you explain the change in auxiliary from *did* to *were*? (Since there is no auxiliary word in the basic sentence, *do* is used to carry the *-ed* affix when the negative is formed. When *be* is introduced as an auxiliary, *do* is no longer required. *Be* + *-ed* = *were*.)

2. In the following sentence, make the transformations requested below the sentence, making the transformations *cumulative*.

> The Acme Corporation is still building houses over on Sixth Avenue.
> a. Passive: (Houses are still being built by the Acme Corporation over on Sixth Avenue. "Over on Sixth Avenue" may also immediately follow "built.")
> b. *There*-expletive: (There are houses still being built by the Acme Corporation over on Sixth Avenue.)

    c. Yes-no question: (Are there houses still being built by
          the Acme Corporation over on Sixth Avenue?)
    d. Negative (-n't): (Aren't there houses still being built by
          the Acme Corporation over on Sixth Avenue?)

Under the *there* transformation, we said that the subject
noun phrase follows *be* as either a main verb or an auxiliary.
In *b* above, does this transformation follow the general
rule? (Yes. The subject follows *are*, the original auxiliary,
though it precedes *being*, which was introduced to form
the passive.)

3. Transform the following basic sentences into their passive
    forms:

    a. Sam turned on the light.
    b. A gang of robbers held up the Denver National Bank.
    c. The scoutmaster crossed several more names off the list.
    d. His lawyer brought this matter up for discussion.
    e. Jim can vouch for my honesty.

    Each of the verbs in the basic sentences is followed by a
    preposition. Does the preposition in every case remain
    with the verb after transformation? (Yes)

    Each preposition—except *up* in sentence *d*—is followed
    by a noun phrase. In which sentences does the noun
    phrase remain with the preposition after transformation?
    (Only in sentence *c*.)

The fact that the prepositions above remain with the verb
rather than with the noun indicates that we do not have the
usual prepositional phrase. The preposition in this case is
called a *particle* and is a part of the verb phrase. Thus we
have these verbs: *turn on, hold up, bring up,* and *vouch for.*

Note, also, that many times a particle may move to the end
of the sentence, rather than remaining in a fixed position between the verb and object: "Sam turned the light *on.*" In which
of the sentences above may the particle *not* be moved in this
way? (Sentence *e*)

In sentence *d* there are two possible passives: "This matter
was brought up for discussion by his lawyer," or "This matter

was brought up by his lawyer *for* discussion." In both cases *up* remains with the verb. Thus *bring up* is a unit.

4. Transform the following basic sentences into their passive forms:
    a. Tony ought to type the letter.
    b. Jim has to patch the tube.
    c. A politician has to put up with all this heckling.
    d. The highway department is going to put a new road through.

    By making each sentence passive, you are able to determine the verb phrase exactly—from modal through any particles. Look at your passive transforms, compare them with the basic sentences, and then write the complete verb phrase for each of the basic sentences. The complete verb phrases are:

    a. ought to type   c. has to put up with
    b. has to patch   d. is going to put through

COMPOUND STRUCTURES IN BASIC SENTENCES

Thus far we have avoided compound structures. But compounds should not raise any serious problems since they seem perfectly natural in sentences like these:

The *dogs and cats* are fighting.
I saw some *lions and tigers*.

When anyone sees two or more kinds of things and introduces them into a sentence, he very naturally uses a compound construction.

A compound structure may be derived from two sentences, like this:

The dogs are fighting.   The cats are fighting.

By deleting the repeated words and introducing a conjunction, we are able to write the compound structure:

The dogs ~~are~~ figh~~t~~ing and (the) cats are fighting.

This example, of course, is very simple, but there are possibilities for conjunction which are not so obvious. Actually, any structure in the sentence can be compound. We can have compound nouns, verbs, predicates, auxiliaries, prepositions, determiners, and so forth. Also, there is a variety of conjunctions that can be used to show exactly the kind of joining desired.

Coordinating conjunctions: and, but, or, nor, for
Correlative conjunctions: either . . . or, neither . . . nor,
    not only . . . but also, both . . . and,
    whether . . . or

Here are a few examples of compound structures:

1. We stayed in our room and studied until nine o'clock.
2. Mr. Jones can and will testify before the committee.
3. The police found neither the gangsters nor the counterfeit money.
4. Jim works both during and after school.

Exercise 1

For each of the following groups of sentences, the student is to (a) write the compound construction which results from combining the sentences, and (b) write the name of the compound structure (noun phrase, predicate, and so forth).

1. The two cowboys rode into town.
   The two cowboys stopped at Canby's saloon.
2. The firemen looked for fire in the second-floor bedrooms.
   The firemen looked for fire in the crawl space beneath the roof.
3. Robert was not studying before dinner.
   Robert was not studying after dinner.
4. Charlotte spilled the cake batter all over her apron.
   Charlotte spilled the cake batter all over her new skirt.
5. The campers tried to pitch their tents in the rain.
   The campers tried to build a fire in the rain.
6. James can help with the paper drive.
   James will help with the paper drive.

7. Sonny ran up the beach looking for shells.
   Sonny ran down the beach looking for shells.
   Sonny did not find any.

Exercise 2

The following newspaper article contains a number of compound structures. The student is to underline each of these compound structures, and above each underlined structure he is to identify the structure (noun phrase, verb phrase, and so forth). Some of these structures contain more than two elements.

An airplane pilot suddenly hears a beeping sound, looks at his dash panel, sees an arrow pointing upward, and swings his craft in that direction.

That, McDonnell Aircraft Corp., said yesterday, is how air collision can be prevented.

McDonnell calls it EROS, for "Eliminate Range Zero System," a device that first warns the pilot his craft is dangerously approaching another airplane, and then shows him what action to take—move up, down, or level off.

EROS gives a 60-second warning at speeds of up to four times the speed of sound and beeps a collision signal at one and a half miles apart for subsonic air speeds.

The Federal Aviation Agency, airline representatives, and military officials have been discussing the collision avoidance device with McDonnell for some time, but no specific production plans have yet been made.

EROS works by radio signals transmitted every two seconds. Calculation of the time delay between transmissions from one plane and reception by another enables the device to measure the distance between planes, the rate of approach, and the altitude of both aircraft. Pilots are told at the same time what to do by up-and-down arrows or a red level-off light in their cabins.*

COMPOUND SENTENCES

Some of the following sentences are basic sentences or simple transforms. Others are combinations of basic sentences and trans-

*Adapted with permission of the Associated Press.

forms written as one sentence. The teacher may wish to write sentences like these on the chalkboard and have volunteers underline each basic sentence and transform, and then draw a circle around any words that join the two separate statements.

1. Some of my friends have gone to the game.
2. The rain fell in torrents all day, and we had to stay inside.
3. Didn't any of the players give you an autograph after the game?
4. There is a roller coaster at the carnival, but I don't want to ride on it.
5. You must lower the sail, for the boat is about to tip over.

Which of those sentences are composed of only one basic sentence or transform? (Sentences 1 and 3.) What is the name of the word used to join each of the pairs of sentences? (Conjunction.) Sentences which are joined together like 2, 4, and 5 above are called *compound sentences*. Each of the constituent sentences making up the compound sentence is called a *clause*.

The following conjunctions are used in the formation of compound sentences:

and	but	for
or	nor	so

Exercise

The student is to rewrite each of the following pairs of sentences as a compound sentence, using one of the conjunctions listed above. He is to use a variety of conjunctions and try not to use *and* every time.

1. Thad planted lettuce seeds in a small plot in the back yard. Nothing came up.
2. Sam should take a taxi to the airport. He will miss his plane.
3. Mrs. Jones took the family car to the garage. She could have the damage repaired right away.
4. Many skyscrapers are being built in our large cities. Some of them have revolutionary new designs.

5. Fred was not accepted by the Marine Corps.
   He did not meet the minimum age requirement.

COORDINATING CONJUNCTIONS

The conjunctions used to join clauses in a compound sentence are called *coordinating conjunctions*. The term *coordinating* indicates that the conjunction joins two clauses which are independent clauses and can function as complete sentences.

Occasionally a complete sentence may begin with a coordinating conjunction, as in:

I waited around for hours. *But* the train never came.

Coordinating conjunctions can show such relationships between clauses as these:

addition—and
contrast—but, yet
alternatives—or, nor
result—so

Usually a comma is used before the conjunction in a compound sentence, but a comma is not used when two phrases are joined. The comma is a signal that the conjunction is occurring at the clause level rather than at the phrase level.

Exercise

The student is to underline each coordinating conjunction in the sentences below. Then above the conjunction he should identify the grammatical units which are being linked together by that conjunction.

                    noun phrases   *verb phrases*
Example: A man *and* three boys stepped out of a car *and*
                                  clauses
        slowly trudged across the field, *but* they soon raced
        back to their car.

1. Most drivers prefer to go through Kentucky and Tennessee, for the scenery is beautiful, and the route is much shorter.
2. Many of those houses, both in the city slums and in the im-

poverished rural areas, should be torn down and replaced by modern houses or apartment buildings.

3. Neither Russia nor the United States wished to fight an all-out war over Cuba and its missile bases, so a satisfactory settlement was arranged by the two great powers.

4. The sentry marched back and forth from one corner of the compound to the other, but he did not look out into the dark fields or the forest beyond.

It is possible, of course, to join more than two sentences together to form a compound sentence. We may form sentences like these:

The temperature dropped sharply, fog rolled in from the bay, and light drizzle saturated the city.

Jet fighters screamed up in a sharp climb, and heavy cargo planes lumbered into the air, but the helicopters lazily rose straight up from their parking ramps.

Students should examine the punctuation of those sentences. How are the two sentences different in the ways they join the three clauses? How are commas used in those structures?

Many times, clauses making up a compound sentence are joined without the use of a coordinating conjunction; a semicolon is used if the writer wishes to unite the two sentences into one compound sentence without using a conjunction. For example:

Will rode in the trailer; Bill drove the car.

When that punctuation is used, we frequently want to insert a *transition* word to indicate the relationship between the two sentences. For example:

$$\text{Will rode in the trailer; } \left. \begin{array}{c} \text{hence} \\ \text{therefore} \\ \text{consequently} \end{array} \right\}, \text{ Bill drove the car.}$$

These are common transition words:

accordingly	hence	nevertheless
also	however	subsequently
besides	in addition	then
consequently	moreover	therefore
furthermore	still	thus

Since the transition words are not grammatically related to either of the constituent sentences, they are punctuated like this:

I don't have my tennis racket unpacked; *moreover,* the weather is too cold for tennis.

The band director doesn't get much encouragement from the school board; *nevertheless,* he turns out some well-trained musicians.

As students have probably observed, the semicolon is much like a weak period. It is halfway between a comma and a period; it is usually not used within a basic sentence for minor tasks like separating items in a series. On the other hand, it is not strong enough to completely separate two sentences. Thus, it often is used to indicate major breaks within compound sentences. For example:

The temperature dropped sharply, fog rolled in from the bay, and light drizzle saturated the city; but brightly lighted cars splashed through the night, and flashing signs told of gay life inside.

Exercise

The student is to combine each of the following groups of sentences into one compound sentence. He should combine sentences by writing both compound phrases and compound sentences, as appropriate. He will probably want to substitute pronouns for some of the repeated nouns. In at least one example he should use a semicolon and transition word.

1. Fred saw a canoe tip over.
   Fred saw two men fall into the lake.
   Fred did not know how to swim.
   Fred could not help them.
2. Mr. Harris poured a cup of steaming coffee.
   Mr. Harris cut a large slice of pie.
   Mr. Harris set his dishes on a tray.
   Mr. Harris walked over to the table.
3. Jim shoveled the sand into the sieve.
   Jim shook the sieve vigorously over a large bucket.
   Jim poured the fine sand into the mortar box.

Jim sloshed in a bucket of water.
Jim added a measure of cement.
Jim worked the mixture with a hoe.

COMPLEX SENTENCES

Although some conjunctions are used to join clauses to form compound sentences, other conjunctions can transform clauses into grammatical units that function much like phrases.

The sentences below are examples of sentences made up of two clauses. Some are compound sentences, but others contain clauses which function as adverbial sub-parts. In each sentence the conjunction that connects the two sentences is italicized.

1. There are three doors in the first room, *and* one of them leads to the dungeon.
2. My neighbor's dog howls *whenever* the moon is shining.
3. The sky remained cloudy all afternoon, *but* there wasn't any rain during the game.
4. He saw a filling station a half mile ahead *just as* his engine stopped.
5. Some burglars broke in and stole jewels from the safe, *yet* the theft was not discovered for several days.

Sentences 2 and 4 are called *complex* sentences because the conjunction changes the structure of one clause and makes it a sub-part of the other clause, much as a phrase is the sub-part of a sentence. The student can see an important difference between the compound sentence and the complex sentence if he tries to place the second clause, complete with its conjunction, in the introductory position, like this:

1. And one of them leads to the dungeon, there are three doors in the first room. (This is not grammatical.)
2. Whenever the moon is shining, my neighbor's dog howls. (This is grammatical.)

Only sentences 2 and 4 above remain grammatically and logically acceptable when they are rearranged by reversing the clauses. Complex sentences often can be rearranged in this way when the second clause has been changed into an adverbial sub-part of the first clause.

Exercise

The student should underline the conjunction which connects the two clauses in the following sentences. Whenever a clause is adverbial, he should write the *some* element which indicates the function of the clause. He should also label each sentence *compound* or *complex*.

1. Phil listened intently to the news broadcast while Harry dashed to a neighboring farmhouse.
2. Emil did not catch very many fish that day, but his wife sold them in the marketplace for a good price.
3. Jim must study in his room every night of the week because he has not been doing well in his classes recently.
4. These rivers will be crowded with fishermen as soon as the fishing season opens.
5. The Mets may not play good baseball, but they draw large crowds game after game.

SUBORDINATE CLAUSES

The clauses which become sub-parts of sentences are called *subordinate clauses*. All the complex sentences above contain subordinate clauses used as adverbials. Here are some additional examples of adverbial subordinate clauses:

Will rode in the trailer *whenever Bill drove the car.*
Will rode in the trailer *while Bill drove the car.*
Will rode in the trailer *because Bill drove the car.*

If we slightly change one of the verbs in the sentences, we can form these other complex sentences:

Will *would ride* in the trailer *if Bill drove the car.*
Will rode in the trailer *so that Bill could drive the car.*
Bill *would not drive* the car *unless Will rode in the trailer.*

The conjunction that is used to form an adverbial subordinate clause is called a *subordinating conjunction*. Subordinating conjunctions are put into a class of conjunctions separate from coordinating conjunctions for these reasons:

    a. The subordinating conjunction, rather than simply joining together clauses, changes one clause into a sub-part of the other, making it function much like a phrase. Thus, in the sentence, "John slept in his room while the storm raged outside," the second clause is an adverbial of time added to the first clause.

    b. The subordinate clause often is a movable adverbial unit, like a basic-sentence adverbial. Therefore, the subordinate clause can appear at the beginning of a sentence. *While the storm raged outside,* John slept in his room. A coordinating conjunction, of course, could not appear in the introductory position and still join the two clauses of a compound sentence.

    c. The subordinating conjunction sometimes requires changes in the verb structure of one of the clauses, as we have already noted.

The adverbial functions of subordinate clauses include:

    a. *Time:* Willy waited *until the fish started biting*.

    b. *Place:* Willy wanted to go *where he could find some excitement*.

    c. *Manner:* Willy hacked at the log *as if he were angry at it*.

    d. *Reason-Purpose:* Willy turned on the light *because he heard strange noises*.

    Willy filled the gas tank *so that he would be ready to leave anytime*.

    e. *Condition:* Willy will read his assignment *if the story is interesting*.

    Willy did not read his assignment *even though the story was interesting*.

Exercise 1

The student should underline the subordinate clause in each of the following sentences and tell which *some* element indicates the function of the clause.

1. Henry picked up a rock and held it over the water as if he intended to splash the young ladies.
2. Tom was not able to repair the bicycle because he did not have any spare parts.
3. If the temperature drops any more, we will not want to go swimming today.
4. Sally washed the dishes in a hurry so that she and Jackie could practice for a few minutes before the tennis match.
5. Before Henrietta sealed the envelope, she inserted a piece of cotton cloth and some buttons.

Exercise 2

The student should write a complex sentence for each pair of sentences below. He may subordinate either one of the sentences. He should transform one of the clauses to function in the adverbial function stated in parentheses.

1. (time) John opened the trunk.
    Several moths fluttered out.
2. (reason-purpose) All of the paper flew off the desk.
    Jane thoughtlessly opened the window.
3. (condition) The coat doesn't fit properly.
    I shall take it back to the store right away.
4. (manner) Dan ran the hundred-yard dash.
    He had a broken leg.
5. (reason-purpose) Alice turned the radio up very loud.
    She could hear it in her room upstairs.

MULTIPLE SUBORDINATE CLAUSES

It is very common for a complex sentence to contain several subordinate clauses. For example:

1. After we had gone several miles, Dad stopped to check the car-top carrier because he could hear the canvas flapping.
2. When Mr. Grumpp puts on his Santa Claus suit, he acts as if he were Santa himself.

3. Harry stayed until the fire was under control because he didn't want it to spread any more.

If we italicize each subordinate clause in the sentences above and substitute the *some* element for the clause, we can see how the subordinate clauses cluster about the main clauses.

1. *Sometime* Dad stopped to check the car-top carrier, *for some reason.*
2. *Sometime* he acts *somehow.*
3. Harry stayed *sometime for some reason.*

The examples above show two separate adverbials in each sentence. Those are simple constructions, but sometimes the structures can become more complicated, as in:

When the frog puffed himself up so that he seemed about to explode, he looked as if he were a foot tall.

If we look at that sentence carefully, we can see that we are putting *two* complex sentences together.

The frog looked as if he were a foot tall.
The frog puffed himself up so that he seemed about to explode.

The second complex sentence is turned into this subordinate clause:

When the frog puffed himself up so that he seemed about to explode, . . .

That building up and interlocking of structures is possible because a subordinate clause is a transform of a basic sentence, and thus it can have its own adverbial sub-parts.

The following sentence is even more complicated.

If you go into the darkroom with me when I am printing pictures, you will have to stay in there until all the pictures are done, because any rays of light can damage the prints while they are in the chemicals.

We can divide that sentence into three complex sentences.

1. You go into the darkroom with me *when I am printing pictures.*

2. You will have to stay in there *until all the pictures are done*.
3. Any ray of light can damage the prints *while they are in the chemicals*.

From that breakdown, we can see the adverbials attached to the proper basic sentences. We can also see how the complex sentences may in turn be transformed into subordinate clauses.

if you go into the darkroom with me when I am printing pictures, . . .
because any ray of light can damage the prints while they are in the chemicals, . . .

Exercise

With the groups of sentences below, the student is to build complex sentences containing adverbial subordinate clauses. He may want to use pronouns in place of repeated noun phrases. He may also rearrange the order of the sentences.

1. Jim will have to practice. (main clause)
   Jim comes out for the baseball team. (time)
   Jim really learns to play second base. (condition)
2. The snow should be removed from all sidewalks. (main clause)
   People will be encouraged to stay off the streets. (reason-purpose)
   The snow has all been removed. (time)
3. The flying saucer rose straight up. (main clause)
   We drew near the flying saucer. (time)
   It was fleeing. (manner)
   We were getting too close. (reason-purpose)

PARTICIPIAL PHRASES

To achieve the greatest effectiveness of expression, we often need to eliminate repetition and wasted motion. For example, the following complex sentences are perfectly good as they stand, but they can be reduced by eliminating unnecessary phrases.

As she stood before the class, the little girl gained confidence.

After he had picked up the evening paper, Father went directly to the living room.

The unnecessary structure in each of those sentences is the repeated subject phrase which we can reduce like this:

Standing before the class, the little girl gained confidence.
Having picked up the evening newspaper, Father went directly to the living room. (or)
After picking up the evening newspaper, Father went directly to the living room.

That type of reduced subordinate clause, in which the verb is changed into an *-ing* form, is called a *participial phrase*.

We take these steps to produce the above participial phrases: (a) We combine two basic sentences to form a complex sentence:

The little girl stood before the class.
The little girl gained confidence.
As she stood before the class, the little girl gained confidence.

(b) *If both basic sentences have the same subject phrase,* we may drop the subject phrase from the subordinate clause, and change the verb of the subordinate clause into a participle (*-ing* form). We usually drop the subordinating conjunction.

Standing before the class, the little girl gained confidence.

The reduction of subordinate clauses is not possible in all complex sentences which have repeating subject phrases. Usually when the subordinate clause is a *time* adverbial (as in the examples above), reduction is possible. Occasionally, clauses in other functions may be reducible, too. For example:

Reason-purpose: *Because he wished to find the source of the quotation,* Sam went to the reference shelf.

Wishing to find the source of the quotation, Sam went to the reference shelf.

Exercise

The student should reduce the subordinate clauses in the following sentences to participial phrases whenever possible. One clause cannot be reduced.

1. As Tom approached the group of men in the road, he gradually slowed down.
2. Because she had already played three straight sets of tennis, Pamela decided to sit out the next set.
3. When John picked up the bat and started toward me, I ran for the dugout.
4. After Pete had taxied to the end of the runway, he applied full throttle and took off.
5. Since John was not a high school graduate, he did not qualify for the job.

PASSIVE PARTICIPIAL PHRASES

Parallel in formation to the participial phrase is the *passive participial phrase,* which can be used in complex sentences to avoid repetition. These two examples show how the complex sentences are formed and how they can be reduced.

1. The soldier was weighted down by his equipment.
   The soldier slogged through the mud.
   Since he was weighted down by his equipment, the soldier slogged through the mud.
   Weighted down by his equipment, the soldier slogged through the mud.
   The soldier, *(being) weighted down by his equipment,* slogged through the mud.

2. The men had been searched for hidden weapons.
   The men were released.
   After the men had been searched for hidden weapons, they were released.
   Having been searched for hidden weapons, the men were released.

To help students understand those reductions, the teacher may wish to ask questions like these:

1. In the clauses which are to be reduced, what is the form of the verb? (passive)
2. Why is this reduction called a *passive participial* phrase?

3. What is the form of the passive participles above? (ends in *-ed*)
4. Can the passive participial phrase take other forms?
5. What would be the passive participial phrase reduction of the subordinate clause in this sentence?

If *the cactus is taken from its natural environment,* it will not grow.

(*Taken* from its natural environment, . . .)

Exercise

The student should reduce the subordinate clauses in the following sentences to either participial phrases or passive participial phrases.

1. When the painting is placed in the bright light, it comes to life.
2. After the artist had placed his painting in the bright light, he pointed to it with pride.
3. Because he was struck by the beauty of the sea, John just wandered along the shore for hours.
4. As soon as he had put all of the books back on the shelf, Mr. Andrews wearily returned to his desk.

INFINITIVE PHRASES

The use of an infinitive phrase is a third means of reducing a subordinate clause to a phrase, as the following reductions illustrate:

John worked all weekend so that he could earn ten dollars.
John worked all weekend *to earn ten dollars.*
So that he can drive to school each day, a student must have his car registered at the school office.
(In order) *to drive to school each day,* a student must have his car registered at the school office.

The teacher may wish to ask questions like these:

1. What is the function of the subordinate clause in each of the above sentences? (reason-purpose)
2. What changes do we make in the structure of the subordinate clause to produce the reduction? (We drop the subor-

dinating conjunction and the repeated subject, and change the verb to its infinitive form—*to* + the base form of the verb. Sometimes *in order to* + the base form of the verb will occur.)

Exercise

The student should reduce the subordinate clauses in the following sentences to infinitive phrases.

1. Phil dived into the pool so that he could save a little girl from drowning.
2. So that you could earn a promotion, you would have to work for the company at least five years.
3. Several students went into the book store so that they could buy their textbooks and writing supplies.

ABSOLUTE PHRASES

The teacher may write the following on the chalkboard so that students can compare these pairs of sentences:

As soon as the professor had finished his lecture, all of the students rushed for the exits.

The professor having finished his lecture, all of the students rushed for the exits.

Because her make-up had been carefully applied, the actress met her fans confidently.

Her make-up having been carefully applied, the actress met her fans confidently.

Then the teacher may ask questions like these:

1. What changes take place in the subordinate clause to produce those reductions?
2. Why isn't the subject phrase in the first sentence dropped from the subordinate clause? (It is not the same as the subject of the main clause.)

Those reductions are called *absolute phrases.* The main difference between an absolute phrase and a participial phrase is that the absolute phrase retains the subject of the subordinate clause, but the participial phrase drops the subject.

Although we have looked at the absolute phrase as a reduction of a subordinate clause, we may show the formation of the phrase from a basic sentence in this way:

$$NP_s + V + rem \text{ (remainder)} \Rightarrow NP_s + \begin{array}{l} V + \text{-ing} \\ V + \text{-en} + rem \end{array}$$

In contrast to the participial and passive participial phrases, that reduction is used when the subject phrase is *not* the same in the two sentences being joined.

Exercise 1

The student should join each of the following pairs of sentences by using an absolute phrase.

1. The crippled airplane had landed safely.
   The fire engine drove away.
2. All the enemy ships had been sunk.
   Old Ironsides returned to the harbor for repairs.
3. The smaller nations were weakened by disagreements.
   It was easy for Rome to conquer them.

Exercise 2

The student should rewrite each of the following groups of sentences, using one of the reductions of a subordinate clause.

1. Jerry walked back and forth across the campus.
   Jerry picked up all of the scraps of paper.
2. The scientists wished to harness the power of the atom.
   The scientists had to perform many dangerous experiments.
3. Their jeep collapsed on the trail.
   The three soldiers carried the supplies the rest of the way on foot.
4. Fred was discovered in the act of taking a puff of his father's cigar.
   Fred very calmly puffed away as if he had always smoked.
5. Wilma lifted the cup to her lips.
   Wilma very gingerly tasted the frothing liquid.

6. Mr. Ryan worked hard all day.
   Mr. Ryan laid the tile on the basement floor.
7. Ken picked up his guitar.
   Ken casually practiced a few chords.
   Ken wanted to loosen up his fingers.
8. The publishers had put much pressure on the authors.
   The authors were to complete their book.
   The three men retreated to the quiet of a hunting lodge.
9. Steve was informed of the praise of the critics.
   Steve bought all of the morning newspapers.
   Steve wanted to read the critics' columns.

ADJECTIVAL CLAUSES

The subordinate clauses which we have been considering build upon a main clause by adding a second sentence to it. This second sentence, when transformed, adds information to the main clause about time, place, manner, purpose, and so on. Subordinate clauses are often movable structures which may appear in introductory, in-sentence, or terminal sentence positions. They are at times reducible to participial, passive participial, infinitive, and absolute phrases.

The next structure we shall examine is also a transformed sentence which is added to a main clause. However, it differs in several ways from the subordinate clauses used as adverbials. To introduce students to this structure, the teacher may wish to write these sentences on the chalkboard and ask the questions that follow.

The boys who are shooting baskets in the gym are preparing for the county tournament.

We are trying to find an air conditioner which will fit into that tiny window.

1. Underline the main clause in each sentence. Place brackets around the subordinate clauses which are not underlined.
2. What is the first word in each of the subordinate clauses? What is the general term we give to such words? (Wh-words: see the discussion of wh-questions, pages 53-57.)

3. Write the basic sentence from which each subordinate clause was derived. (The boys are shooting baskets in the gym. An air conditioner will fit into that tiny window.)
4. What changes take place when these two basic sentences are transformed into the subordinate clauses? (The subject noun phrase is replaced by a wh-word.)
5. Try moving the subordinate clauses into other sentence positions. Are these clauses movable? (No.)
6. Why would these clauses *not* be movable? (The wh-word refers back to the noun just preceding it.)

In our first examples, the wh-words function as subjects of the subordinate clauses. The wh-word can also perform any of the several functions of noun phrases. For example:

1. The trips *which Sam and I are planning* will take us up into Canada.
2. The house *which Ted used to live in* was haunted.
3. Several of the girls *whom the director interviewed* were hired for bit parts.

Each of those adjectival clauses has its subject phrase *following* the wh-word. If we wish to determine the function of the wh-word in any of those sentences, we should look at the structure of the sentence *before* it was transformed to an adjectival clause. For example, for sentence 1 we would have this sentence:

Sam and I are planning *the trips*.

Then we determine the function of the recurring noun phrase, *the trips,* which in this case is an *object*. The wh-word in the transform has the same function as the noun phrase in the untransformed sentence.

The teacher may ask students these questions:

1. What is the function of the wh-word in sentence 2? (object of preposition)
2. What is the function of the wh-word in sentence 3? (object)
3. In sentence 3, why does the form *whom* occur instead of *who*?
4. In sentences 1 and 2, could *whom* be used instead of *which*? Why?

Those subordinate clauses all provide additional information about a noun in the main clause. It is logical, therefore, to call them *adjectival clauses.*

The transformation that produces an adjectival clause regularly introduces one of the wh-words. Therefore, we may also call the transform a *wh-clause.* But, since the wh-clause is used in a variety of structures, we shall refer to the clauses in this section as adjectival clauses.

From the few example sentences so far, we can make these observations about the derivation, structure, and position of the subordinate clauses which function as adjectivals:

a. One sentence may enter another sentence as an adjectival clause if the same noun occurs in both sentences.
b. The adjectival clause is a transform which replaces the recurring noun phrase with a wh-word, and places the wh-word in the initial position in the transform. The adjectival clause begins with a wh-word regardless of the function of the wh-word.
c. The adjectival clause immediately follows the recurring noun phrase of the main clause.

We can note a significant difference between the transformations which produce the adverbial clause and the adjectival clause. In the adverbial clause, a wh-word *precedes* the sentence to be transformed.

Jack made the trip ⇒ ... *when* Jack made the trip

In the adjectival clause, a wh-word *replaces* a phrase in the sentence to be transformed.

Jack made the trip ⇒ ... *which* Jack made

Exercise 1

For each of the following groups of sentences, the student should write a complex sentence containing an adjectival clause. He should follow this procedure: (a) Underline the noun phrase that occurs in both sentences; then place a caret (∧) in the first sentence at the position where the second sentence may enter. (b) Write the transform of the second sentence. (c) Write the final complex sentence.

> Example: *The trees* ∧ blocked the highway.
>   *The trees* had been blown down in the storm.
> Transform: which had been blown down in the storm
> Complex sentence: The trees which had been blown down in
>   the storm blocked the highway.

1. The sandbar is a danger to navigation.
   The sandbar is only a few inches below the surface.
   Transform:
   Complex sentence:
2. The tests have not been graded.
   We took the tests last Thursday.
   Transform:
   Complex sentence:
3. The student has become a famous doctor.
   The teachers are talking about the student.
   Transform:
   Complex sentence:

It is possible to insert more than one adjectival clause into a sentence. For example:

> Main clause: The sailors climbed into the lifeboats.
> Sentences to be inserted:
>   The sailors made a final check of all the staterooms.
>   The lifeboats were not crowded.
> Complex sentence:
>   The sailors *who had made a final check of all the staterooms*
>   climbed into the lifeboats *which were not crowded.*

The teacher may wish to ask questions like these:

1. What conditions make it possible for us to put two adjectival clauses into that main clause? (Each sentence to be inserted makes a statement about a different noun phrase; therefore, each subordinate clause follows a different noun phrase.)

2. Would it be possible to transform the following two sentences into adjectival clauses and insert them into the main clause above?

> The sailors had made a final check of all the staterooms.
> The sailors had shut off the engines.

Why is it difficult to insert both of those sentences into the main clause? (They both have to go into the same sentence position; the wh-word of one clause cannot occur next to the appropriate noun phrase. However, the two clauses can be inserted if they are written as a *compound* structure. For example:

> The sailors *who had made a final check of all the staterooms and (who) had shut off the engines* climbed into the lifeboats.)

Thus, we can see that *one* adjectival clause can follow *any* noun in the main clause. But, because each adjectival transform must immediately follow the appropriate noun phrase, it is unlikely that multiple clause inserts will occur in a single position.

The teacher may find that a diagram will help to clarify the concepts involved in the use of adjectival clauses. We may show the derivation of the complex sentence above by means of a diagram, like this:

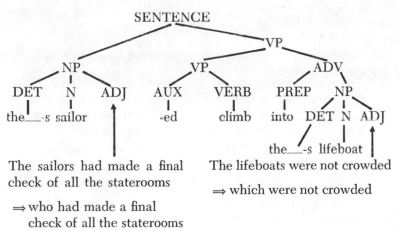

The sailors had made a final check of all the staterooms

⇒ who had made a final check of all the staterooms

The lifeboats were not crowded

⇒ which were not crowded

Such a diagram shows that the adjectival clause is inserted as a *sub-part of the noun phrase*. The same noun phrase must occur in the main clause and in the sentence to be inserted; the adjectival clause must immediately follow the recurring noun phrase.

Exercise 2

The following sentences are to be main clauses in a complex sentence. The student is to make up sentences about the nouns italicized in the main clause. Then he should write a complex sentence by transforming the sentences which he has made up and inserting them into the main clause.

>   Example: *The pools of water* are breeding places for *insects.*
>   The pools of water are scattered around the vacant lots.
>   Insects carry diseases.
>   Complex sentence:
>   The pools of water which are scattered around the lots are breeding places for insects which carry diseases.

  1. *The cars* will travel down *the road.*
  2. *The waves* have washed away *much of the land.*
  3. *The photographs* tell of *a country.*

THAT CLAUSES

So far we have used only three different wh-words in transforming sentences into adjectival clauses:

>   who—replaces nouns with human referents when the
>   wh-word functions as subject or subject complement
>   whom—replaces nouns with human referents when the
>   wh-word functions as object, indirect object,
>   object complement, or object of preposition
>   which—replaces nouns with non-human referents

But we also find that three other words are commonly used in forming adjectival clauses.

The following sentences show adjectival clauses introduced by *that:*

1. The briefcase that Jim was carrying contained important documents.
2. I didn't recognize the man that delivered the message.
3. The boy that you are referring to works for a printing firm.

The teacher may wish to ask questions like these:

1. Which word in those sentences is used in the same way that a wh-word is used? (that)
2. Which wh-word might have been used in sentence 1? (which)
3. Which wh-word might have been used in sentence 2? (who)
4. Which wh-word might have been used in sentence 3? (whom)
5. Just from looking at these three sentences, how would you say that *that* can be used in adjectival clauses? (As an alternative form of the wh-words—with either human or non-human referents, for either subject or object functions.)

While *that* is widely used as an alternative for *who* and *whom,* many people prefer to use *who* and *whom* when referring to human beings. But there is no clear distinction in usage between *that* and *which.*

Frequently in an adjectival clause we need to use a wh-word as a substitute for some sentence sub-part other than a noun phrase. For example:

1. We want to hire a man whose training is especially strong in mathematics and science.
2. Sam lives in the house where I was born.
3. That was the only time when I was really scared.

The teacher may wish to ask questions like these:

1. What is the wh-word in sentence 1? (whose)
   Why is that particular wh-word used? (Possessive form—replaces the possessive noun, *"a man's* training is . . . ")
2. What is the wh-word in sentence 2? (where)
   Why is that particular wh-word used? (It replaces an ad-

verbial of place—the prepositional phrase, "I was born in the house.")

3. Which wh-word would be used if the preposition were retained in the adjectival clause? (which—". . . the house *which* I was born *in*," or ". . . the house *in which* I was born.")

4. What is the wh-word in sentence 3? (when)
   Why is that particular wh-word used? (It replaces an adverbial of time—the prepositional phrase, "I was scared *at the time*.") Which wh-word would be used if the preposition were retained in the adjectival clause? (which—". . . the only time *at which* I was scared.")

Then students should examine sentences like these:

1. The lady I was talking to asked me to run an errand for her.
2. Mrs. Lewis has not read the article you wrote for the school newspaper.
3. The problems Jim encountered only drove him on to greater effort.

The adjectival clauses in the above sentences are:

1. I was talking to
2. you wrote for the school paper
3. Jim encountered

How do students account for the absence of wh-words in these transforms? (The wh-words were dropped because they were not necessary in expressing the idea in the sentence.)

If we write the transforms with their wh-words included, we have:

1. *whom* I was talking to
2. *which* you wrote for the school paper
3. *which* Jim encountered

The function of each of those wh-words is (1) object of preposition, (2) object, and (3) object. It is not possible to drop the wh-word when it functions as the subject, as in these sentences:

1. You should close all the windows *which* are open.
2. Everyone has great respect for the soldier *who* fights to defend his country.

3. The pitcher *who* injured his arm was put on the disabled list.

The wh-word usually may be deleted if it functions as one of the objects, but not if it functions as the subject.

Exercise

For each group of sentences below, the student should write one complex sentence. He should use adjectival clause transforms for all sentences to be inserted.

1. The black clouds looked ominous to the players.
   The black clouds towered high in the sky.
   The players had just run onto the field.
2. The golfer spent ten minutes looking through the grove of trees.
   The golfer was playing in front of Fred.
   The golfer had lost a new ball in the grove of trees.
3. Any man would be angry at the insulting questions.
   Any man's sense of honor is strong.
   The lawyer is asking the insulting questions.

REDUCED ADJECTIVAL CLAUSES

When we studied adverbial clauses, we observed that often a part of a clause can be omitted if the adverbial clause and the main clause have the same subject. We saw that participial and infinitive phrases are produced when we reduce the adverbial clauses.

Similar reductions can be made of adjectival clauses. For example:

That man who is standing over there looks very familiar.
   (becomes)
That man standing over there looks very familiar.

Reductions of adjectival clauses can, in addition, produce several other structures. For example:

1. All students who have been chosen for the school band will rehearse at two o'clock.

   2. Several packages which were left in the hallway have disappeared.
   3. The novel which is entitled *Brave New World* gives a pessimistic view of our future.
   4. My friend who is named Pierre is going to move to California.
   5. All men admire the missionary-doctor who was Albert Schweitzer.

In sentences 1 and 2 what words can be omitted from the adjectival clauses? What is the name of the reduction? (passive participle)

In sentences 3, 4, and 5 what words can be omitted from the adjectival clauses?

Students should recognize that sentences 1 and 2 have the same structure as the passive participles that we earlier saw being used as reductions of adverbial clauses. However, the reductions of 3, 4, and 5 illustrate a reduction which we have not studied previously. In structure, each reduction is a noun phrase, and it has the same referent as the preceding noun phrase. It is called an *appositive*. This diagram shows how the appositive in sentence 3 enters the noun phrase:

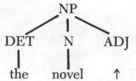

          The novel is entitled *Brave New World*
          ⇒ which is entitled *Brave New World*

Exercise

The student should write each of the following groups of sentences as a complex sentence, using adjectival clause transforms of sentences to be inserted into the main clause. Then, wherever possible, he should reduce each of the transforms to a participial phrase, passive participial phrase, or appositive.

Example: That signboard is about to fall.

That signboard is projecting out over the street.

That signboard, which is projecting out over the street, is about to fall.

That signboard projecting out over the street is about to fall.

1. The pilot let my brother go up into the cockpit.
   My brother is Fred.
2. The curator is proud of the artifacts.
   The curator works for our city museum.
   The artifacts were found by his latest expedition.
3. The scientist looked into his microscope and saw the little animals.
   The scientist was Leeuwenhoek.
   The little animals were swimming around in a drop of water.
4. Any records will be kept in a place.
   Any records are seized by the police.
   They will be safe in the place.
5. Anyone would be very foolish not to use seatbelts.
   Anyone is riding along a turnpike at high speeds.
   The seatbelts have been installed in the car.

NOMINAL CLAUSES

Both the adverbial clauses and the adjectival clauses are transforms which are *optional additions* to main clauses. Now we are ready to look at transforms which help to form the basic structure of the main clause. These transforms function in the same way as noun phrases and are called *nominal* clauses.

In the following sentences, each clause used as a noun has been italicized and labeled according to its function.

Obj
1. Sara knew *that I had hidden the box of candy.*

Obj
2. All of those boys should have realized *that the track team was practicing this afternoon.*

sc
3. The problem is *that Tom cannot learn his part in the play.*

subj
4. *That the little boy had lost his way* seemed very probable.

Since a nominal clause functions in its sentence as a single grammatical unit, it can be replaced by the word *something*. For example, the sentences above could be rewritten like this:

1. Sara knew *something.*
2. All of those boys should have realized *something.*
3. The problem is *something.*
4. *Something* seemed very probable.

We find it helpful to substitute *something* for the nominal clause for two reasons: (a) we can verify that the clause actually is a nominal unit if *something* is an acceptable replacement, and (b) we can determine the function of the clause much more easily when it is reduced to a single word.

It may be helpful to students to see the derivational diagram of a sentence containing a nominal clause. Sentences 3 and 4 above may be diagramed like this:

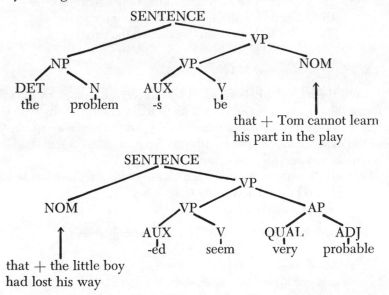

Exercise 1

Each of the following sentences contains a nominal clause. The student should rewrite the sentences, substituting *something* for the nominal clauses. Then he should indicate the function of *something*, i.e., the function of the nominal clause.

1. The professor will assume that everyone has completed the assignment.
2. The principal danger is that drivers will become careless.
3. That these shoes are beyond repair is perfectly obvious.

Exercise 2

The student should combine each of the following pairs of sentences to form a complex sentence containing a nominal clause. The word *something* shows the position in the main clause where the nominal clause should be placed.

1. The world recognizes *something*.
   Dr. Schweitzer lived a very inspiring life.
2. His conclusion seemed to be *something*.
   The National League must expand to include one more franchise.
3. *Something* is the inevitable result.
   Our lakes will become completely polluted.

There are several other nominal transforms in addition to the *that*-clause. For example:

1. Sam didn't know *when the meeting started*.
2. *Why Bill asked that question* has been bothering me all day.
3. The astronaut would not talk about *what happened during his second orbit*.
4. The lieutenant will decide *who is to be promoted*.

We observe that *something* can be substituted for each of the italicized clauses. What is the function of the clause in sentence 3? (Object of preposition.) How would you describe the structure of these transforms? (Wh-word + sentence, or sentence beginning with a wh-word.) What other transforms are the same, or similar, in structure to this transform? (The wh-question, some adverbial clauses, the adjectival clauses. For example:

> Sam was there *when the meeting started* [adverbial clause].
>
> *Why did Bill ask that question?* [wh-question. This transform also involves putting the auxiliary ahead of the subject phrase].
>
> Anyone *who is to be promoted* must get a new identification card [adjectival clause].)

The wh-transform is a vital part of many grammatical structures in English. The *wh-clause,* which we observed earlier in our discussion of adjectival clauses, is very commonly used as a nominal. Now let us examine these sentences:

1. The citizens of Tombstone object to *the outlaw's shooting up their town.*
2. *His giving money to that organization* seemed ironic.

Again, *something* may be substituted for the italicized transforms. What would be the basic sentence from which each of the italicized clauses was transformed?

1. The outlaw shoots up their town.
2. He gave money to that organization.

What structural change takes place in producing that transform? (The subject takes the possessive form; the verb takes the *-ing* form.)

We may show, in a very simple way, the transformation which produces the above nominal structures:

$$NP_s + V + \text{remainder} \Rightarrow NP_s + \text{-'s} + V + \text{-ing} + \text{remainder}$$

The transform which we see in those sentences is called a *gerund phrase,* which frequently appears in a somewhat simpler form. For example:

1. *Bringing an airplane down safely* involves a great deal of skill.

2. Harold thought about *buying a house in the country*.
   Can *something* be used to replace the underlined phrases?
   (yes)
   How do those transforms differ from the gerund phrases we
   saw in sentence 2 above? (The N_s + -'s is omitted.)
   Why isn't there a subject expressed for either of those gerunds? (In sentence 1, the subject is simply understood; a
   pilot is the logical one to bring a plane down safely. In sentence 2, the same subject occurs both in the main clause
   and in the sentence to be inserted.
   Harold thought about *something*.
   Harold buys a house in the country.)

The briefest form of the gerund phrase is a phrase in which only
the verb + -ing appears, like this:

1. *Skiing* is a very exciting sport.
   Something is a very exciting sport.
   Someone skis.
2. Dad's favorite pastime is *reading*.
   Dad's favorite pastime is *something*.
   Dad reads (books, magazines, and so forth).

There are other transforms used as nominals, but this brief review of *that-clauses, wh-clauses,* and *gerund phrases* may at least
suggest the kinds of structures possible.

Exercise

For each group of sentences below, the student should write a
complex sentence containing one or more nominal transforms. He
should use the transform requested in parentheses.

Example: *Something* was *something*.
Some road goes to Cornwall. (wh-clause)
I wanted to know something. (wh-clause)
Which road leads to Cornwall was what I wanted
to know.

1. *Something* gives me back pains.
   I sleep on a lumpy mattress. (gerund phrase)

2. The people of this state would like to know *something*.
   The governor entered the New Hampshire primaries *for some reason*. (wh-clause)

3. *Something* makes his parents wonder *something*.
   Tom earned all D's on his report card. (that-clause)
   He studied *so much*. (wh-clause)

4. I think *something*.
   Most of these people know *something*. (that-clause)
   Something is expected of them. (wh-clause)

5. *Something* was *something*.
   The driving instructor criticized you for *something*.
      (wh-clause)
   You failed to slow down at the intersection. (gerund phrase)

Grade Nine

This program for grade nine begins with a brief review of the major concepts presented in grades seven and eight. The review consists of a series of exercises designed to refresh the memories of students and to ferret out areas of weakness for further study. A few questions usually follow each exercise. Some questions require only brief, factual answers; others inquire deeply into grammatical structures and transformational processes. We hope that the questions will prompt students to think carefully about their language, to draw upon their own experiences with language, and to formulate basic language principles in their own terms.

REVIEW FOR GRADE NINE

Review Exercise 1

The student is asked to draw diagonal lines between form-word phrases and to indicate the form class, i.e., N, V, or Adj, beneath each phrase.

Example: A student / broke / the world's record.
          N   V   N

1. Each car has been waxed.
2. The front porch of Mr. Maxey's house looks very rickety.
3. Our whole class ought to send Miss Bloom a thank-you note.
4. You should look up her telephone number.
5. The first day of the week brought good weather.
6. My grass has turned brown.
7. Last night's rain washed out the ocelot's tracks.
8. Hot cocoa smells good.

9. Several of those angry men could have torn up the town.
10. Many of those ninth graders of yours may become very good grammarians.

QUESTIONS

a. How is the word *of* used in sentences 2, 5, 9, and 10?
b. What do we call these structures: *Mr. Maxey's* (sentence 2), *last night's* (sentence 7), and *of yours* (sentence 10)?
c. What is the name of the structure words that pattern with a noun? What is the name of the structure words that pattern with a verb? What is the name of the structure words that pattern with an adjective?
d. How are these words used: *up* (sentence 4), *out* (sentence 7), and *up* (sentence 9)?
e. Which of the noun phrases in the sentences above contain adjectives?
f. Which modals appear in the sentences above? List all past participles that appear in those sentences.
g. When is a past participle form used in the verb phrase?

Review Exercise 2

The student is asked to draw diagonal lines between the form-word phrases and then write the form and function, i.e., N_s, V_{tr}, N_o, and Adj_{sc}, beneath each phrase.

Example: Sarah's Siamese cat / has eaten / the roast.
$$N_s \qquad\qquad V_{tr} \qquad\qquad N_o$$

1. My pet ocelot frightens people.
2. A few of these geometry books have no covers.
3. One group of five Cub Scouts is about to start a fire.
4. The clubhouse became a shambles.
5. Grandma's doughnuts taste very spicy.
6. One of the students should have looked sick.
7. Martha Smith's brother has given his teacher an apple.
8. A few of the lions have escaped.
9. Some actors might call that director a genius.
10. Several more of those Christmas bulbs will burn out.

QUESTIONS

   a. Which noun phrases contain a second noun in addition to the head-noun of the phrase?
   b. What is the tense of the verb in each of these sentences: 1, 4, 7, and 10?
   c. Why does the auxiliary word *has* occur in sentence 7, while *have* occurs in sentence 2?
   d. How can you distinguish between the sentence patterns in sentences 7 and 9?

Review Exercise 3

The student is asked to underline each adverbial in the sentences below and to tell which *some* element it replaces.

   1. Your cousin should wait on the porch.
   2. Bill counted the cards rapidly.
   3. The car has rusted badly under the chrome.
   4. Last Tuesday the class went to the museum.
   5. After the shot, one of the detectives ran up the stairs.
   6. Before class, Mary looked up his telephone number.
   7. During Miss Bloom's demonstration, Leo hid his comic book carefully inside his notebook.
   8. After his dancing lesson this afternoon, Wilbur will hang that picture on the wall.
   9. All night long the dogs eagerly chased the convict through the woods.
   10. The climbers cut footholds in the ice every few feet all the way to the top of the mountain.

QUESTIONS

   a. Which of the above sentences seem incomplete if they are uttered without adverbials?
   b. In which sentence positions can an adverbial occur?
   c. When two or more adverbials occur in a sentence, is there a regular sequence in which they occur? What sequences do you find in the sentences above?

Review Exercise 4

The student is asked to underline each adverbial in the sentences below, to tell which *some* element it replaces, and to name its form class.

1. After class most of the students angrily threw their test papers into the wastebasket.
2. Tomorrow night after the movie we shall go home on the subway.
3. Suddenly Joe dashed across the street to the camera store for some more flashbulbs.
4. Some athletes have to run ten miles every day for months at a time.

QUESTIONS

a. Look carefully at the forms and *some* elements of the adverbials in the sentences above. Do certain forms and *some* elements occur together regularly? If so, which ones?
b. Rewrite each of those sentences by rearranging the adverbials into another acceptable order.

Review Exercise 5

Each of the sentences below is a transform. The student is asked to give the information requested after each transform.

Example: Has the player signed his contract?
    a. Basic sentence: The player has signed his contract.
    b. Structural change: Move the auxiliary to the position ahead of the subject phrase.
    c. Name of the transform: yes-no question

1. Pick up that piece of paper.
    a. Basic sentence:
    b. Structural change:
    c. Name of transform:
2. Did Elmer repair the hole in the roof yesterday?
    a. Basic sentence:
    b. Structural change:
    c. Name of transform:

3. A great many of the students have not been able to finish the test.
   a. Basic sentence:
   b. Structural change:
   c. Name of transform:

4. There may be more than one correct answer.
   a. Basic sentence:
   b. Structural change:
   c. Name of transform:

5. When did the football team hold its last practice?
   a. Basic sentence:
   b. Structural change:
   c. Name of transform:

6. Most of the painting was done by a crew of men from Jim's Hardware Store.
   a. Basic sentence:
   b. Structural change:
   c. Name of transform:

Note: The following sentences contain more than one transform in each sentence.

7. There were not very many strawberries in the garden.
   a. Basic sentence:
   b. Structural change:
   c. Name of transforms:

8. Haven't some of the planes been damaged by the hurricane?
   a. Basic sentence:
   b. Structural change:
   c. Name of transforms:

9. Shouldn't there be mail deliveries both morning and afternoon?
   a. Basic sentence:
   b. Structural change:
   c. Name of transforms:

10. Why haven't there been more bills passed during this session of Congress?
    a. Basic sentence:
    b. Structural change:
    c. Name of transforms:

Review Exercise 6

The student is asked to underline each conjunction and to write below it the form of the structures that it connects.

Example: The three boys saw *but* did not talk to the governor.
verb phrase

1. Neither the chief of police nor his assistant could be located.
2. There probably will not be any trout or bass in that lake.
3. Sam is in and out of the office all day long.
4. A herd of elk gracefully bounded through the woods and across the field.
5. Most of the children were either arguing or complaining all afternoon.
6. Why don't you spend the money for a tent, sleeping bag, and cooking kit?
7. Fred started down into the cave, but no one followed him.
8. The wrecking crew set up their equipment, great steel balls crushed the walls, and the tired old building collapsed.
9. Either you bring the lawn mower back, or I'll come over after it.
10. The Adamses should hire a boy to cut the lawn, for they will be out of town nearly all summer.
11. I don't agree with Mr. Tufts' remarks, yet I defend his right to speak out on the issue.
12. You should plant the tulips and daffodils this fall, but do not plant the begonias until spring.

QUESTIONS

a. Make a list of all the different conjunctions used in those sentences. What name do we give to those conjunctions?
b. What grammatical structures can be made compound?

Review Exercise 7

The student is asked to underline each adverbial clause in the following sentences and to tell which *some* element the clause replaces.

1. Ken didn't want to leave the game while the score was tied.
2. The grass grows better over there because the ground is moist.
3. Even though the boat looks perfectly safe, I shall put on my life jacket.
4. Whenever the waves beat up against the shore, they wash away a little more of the soil.
5. Mushrooms will grow best where it is cool, shady, and damp.
6. Charlie left his telephone number so that you could call him when you came back.
7. Ever since Jean spent that summer in Europe, she has felt as if the old home town is just too small and dull for her.
8. Sally and Sue, as we might expect, sneaked out the door as soon as Miss Cross went back to the kitchen.
9. If the horses are not properly broken in before we buy them, we shall have to keep Jim on the staff until they are trained.
10. Although the car looks new at this moment, it will not look that way very long unless you keep it clean.

QUESTIONS

a. How do you describe the *structure* of the adverbial clause?
b. List each of the subordinators from the above sentences under the correct heading:

Adverbial *of time*	Adverbial *of place*	Adverbial *of manner*
Adverbial of *reason-purpose*	Adverbial *of condition*	Other? _____

c. What rules of punctuation can you formulate from the above examples?

Review Exercise 8

The student is asked to underline each reduced adverbial clause in the following sentences. Then he is (a) to write the full adverbial clause, and (b) to write the name of the phrase—participial phrase, passive participial phrase, infinitive phrase, or absolute phrase.

> Example: *Filing through the stately halls of the capitol,* the students were very much impressed by the building.
>
> 1. as the students filed through the stately halls of the capitol
> 2. participial phrase

1. To support his argument, the speaker quoted statistics from *The New York Times.*
2. His hat jauntily tipped to one side, Bill strode through the crowd of admirers.
3. Though unaccustomed to such luxury and service, the farm boy enjoyed his first commercial flight.
4. Don, his head heavily bandaged and both legs in casts, was wheeled into the doctor's office.
5. Several students, wishing to make an impression on their new teacher, turned in their test papers early.
6. The mayor maintained his good humor and even temper, even while being criticized for certain errors in judgment.
7. Being a sensitive person, the poet selected his words carefully to convey exactly the right emotion. (There can be more than one adverbial in a sentence.)
8. Inspired by the bright morning, Mr. Downs, humming a merry tune, stepped up to the practice green to try a few putts.

QUESTIONS

a. What conditions are necessary to produce a participial phrase reduction of an adverbial clause?
b. What conditions are necessary to produce a passive participial phrase reduction of an adverbial clause?
c. What conditions are necessary to produce an infinitive-phrase reduction of an adverbial clause?
d. What conditions are necessary to produce an absolute-phrase reduction of an adverbial clause?

Review Exercise 9

(A reminder: An adjectival clause is grammatically a sub-part of a noun phrase. We may show this relationship by a simple diagram:

The sentence which enters the ADJ position must contain the same noun as N in the noun phrase. Then the recurring noun becomes a wh-word in the adjectival-clause transform. For example:

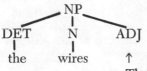

The *wires* were blown down by the wind.
. . . *which* were blown down by the wind.)

The student is asked to underline each adjectival clause, and then to draw a circle around the noun in the main clause which recurs in the adjectival clause (as the wh-word). Finally, he is to write the original sentence from which the adjectival-clause transform was derived.

> Example: The (wires) *which were blown down by the wind* were repaired within a few hours.
>
> The wires were blown down by the wind.

1. One of the architects who designed the building is overseeing its construction.
2. There is a boy in our class whose Dad is an atomic scientist.
3. One of the actors whom Mr. James interviewed is suing the newspaper for one million dollars.
4. The shipwrecked sailors caught a little of the rain that fell during the night.
5. That television set which Mr. Killian bought is completely worthless.

6. The play that we attended in Cleveland last week was the first stage production I have ever seen.
7. The shack which the children are using for a playhouse is situated on the plot of land where the Smiths plan to build their house.
8. The pastries you enjoy so much are made only on the weekends when Mrs. Baker fills in for a vacationing employee.
9. No one has given any reason why the water that we are drinking is so bitter and rusty.
10. The man who drove the car that broke the course record wants to see the movies that you took during the race.

QUESTIONS

a. How would you describe the structure of an adjectival clause?
b. Tell why each of the following wh-words is used:
   Sentence 2—whose
   Sentence 3—whom
   Sentence 7—where
   Sentence 8—when
   Sentence 9—why
c. In which adjectival clauses is *that* substituted for the wh-word? Under what conditions is it possible to make this substitution?
d. Which two adjectival clauses omit the wh-word entirely? Under what conditions is it possible to omit the wh-word?

Review Exercise 10

The theory: All adjectival structures are considered to be derived from adjectival clauses. Thus we have the following derivations:

Adjectival Clause	*Reduction*
1. The boy *who wrote the best essay* won the prize.	no reduction
2. The boy *who is sitting over there* won the prize.	*sitting over there*

3. The boy *who was chosen by the committee* won the prize.   *chosen by the committee*
4. The boy *who is in the front seat* won the prize.   *in the front seat*
5. Tom Adams, *who is my best friend,* won the prize.   *my best friend*
6. A boy *who is very clever* won the prize.   a *very clever* boy

a. What words are omitted in the formation of each reduction? What general rule might you make about forming the reductions of adjectival clauses?
b. Write the name which identifies each of the above reductions:

2. _____
3. _____
4. _____
5. _____
6. _____

c. In all of those reductions except sentence 6, the reduction *follows* the noun phrase. But it is possible for some of those reductions to *precede* the noun. For example:

1. The firemen directed a stream of water at the house *which was burning.* The firemen directed a stream of water at the *burning* house.
2. A bureau covered the wall *which was damaged.* A bureau covered the *damaged* wall.

What conditions are required for a participial or passive-participial phrase to precede a noun?

In the following sentences, the student is asked to underline *completely* each noun phrase which contains any adjectival elements. He should place parentheses around all adjectival clauses and reductions of adjectival clauses which are sub-parts of a noun phrase. Then he is to write the name of the reduction beneath it.

Example: *Several of the (tall) boys (on our basketball team)*
     adj. phrase   prep. phrase
  are getting scholarships.

1. I just met a very pretty girl who has transferred to our school from a school in Japan.
2. That green upholstered chair in your room would be just right for my room.
3. The tramp looked through the window at a pot of black coffee steaming on the stove.
4. One of Fred's best friends, a policeman from Zenith who builds his own ham radio sets, received an SOS message from an ocean liner.
5. Two gleaming white sedans decorated with flashing beacons raced through the intersection.

Review Exercise 11

(A reminder: A nominal clause is a unit which functions like a noun phrase. Therefore, we can substitute the word *something* for a nominal clause. For example, in the sentence "One of the actors decided that those lines should be cut from the play," we might substitute the word *something* like this: "One of the actors decided *something*.")

The student is asked to underline each nominal clause in the sentences below. Then he should write the clause's function in the main clause.

               Obj
Example: One of the actors decided *that those lines should be cut from the play.*

1. Our main problem is that the racing shell is very long and fragile.
2. That most people in the world want peace is unquestionable.
3. The speaker apparently was worried about how the audience would react to his message.
4. It is not likely that Tim would intentionally tear up the theme. (*It* in this sentence is an *expletive*. *It* is used as a

filler word for a nominal clause, as *there* is used as a filler word for NP in the transform of a basic sentence.)

5. What the workers should do in case of an air raid is the subject of our discussion tonight.

6. I doubt that William knows why we are having the special election.

7. It is not clear to me who is supposed to decide whether the game is to be played or not. (See the note to sentence 4.)

8. I think the sergeant has found out where you hid his new boots.

9. How the monkeys escaped from the cage is what we want to find out.

QUESTIONS

a. Each nominal clause (except one) is introduced by a special word. Make a list of those words. Which nominal clause is *not* introduced by such a word? What word *might* have been used?

b. What are the two main structures that occur as nominal clauses? How would you describe each of those structures?

c. Sentences 4 and 7 begin with the expletive *it*. What structural changes take place when the *expletive-it* transform occurs? Point out the parallels between the *expletive-there* and the *expletive-it* transformations.

d. Which sentences contain more than one nominal clause?

e. What is the verb of the main clause in sentence 9?

f. Write the original sentence from which each nominal clause has been derived. For the example sentence, we would write: "Those lines should be cut from the play."

Review Exercise 12

(A reminder: We may use *something* as a substitute for a reduced nominal clause as we did in the last exercise for nominal clauses.)

The student is asked to underline each reduced nominal clause in the sentences below. Then he should write the original sentence from which the nominal structure was derived.

Example: Some of the players objected to *Sam's using a first-baseman's glove in the outfield.*
Sam used a first-baseman's glove in the outfield.

1. The governor's pardoning those prisoners earned him much good will.
2. The biggest mistake was Bob's putting all the food in one pack.
3. Driving across the George Washington Bridge makes me nervous.

QUESTIONS

a. What is the name of the reduced nominal clause in each of the sentences above? (gerund phrase)
b. How do you explain the occurrence of the possessive nouns in sentences 1 and 2? (The gerund transform: N_s + V + remainder $\Rightarrow$ N_s + -'s + V + -ing + remainder)
c. Why isn't there a possessive noun in sentence 3? (The same noun occurs in both the main clause and the reduced clause; thus the noun is not repeated in the reduced clause.)
d. Write the function of each reduced nominal clause in the sentences above.

In addition to the gerund phrase, we may use infinitive phrases as nominals. (Though we did not study the infinitive as a nominal transform in grade eight, a student of grammar should be able to work out this problem.) Infinitive phrases, like gerund phrases, are reduced nominal clauses. In each of the following sentences, the student should underline the infinitive phrase functioning as a nominal and then write the sentence from which the infinitive phrase was derived.

1. John did not try to finish the job on time.
2. It is very difficult for a camel to pass through the eye of a needle.
3. Sally doesn't know how to mingle freely with people.
4. To drive through the heart of the city would take us three hours.
5. David always knows what to do in an emergency.

These are the sentences from which the infinitive phrases are derived:

1. John finishes the job on time.
2. A camel passes through the eye of a needle.
3. Sally mingles freely with people somehow.
4. We drive through the heart of the city.
5. David does something in an emergency.

The student should look carefully at the forms of these infinitive phrases.

In sentences 1 and 4, the phrase in each sentence starts with the infinitive: *to finish* and *to drive*. In these sentences, a noun phrase in the main clause is the "understood" subject of the infinitive phrase. Since it is clear who or what would be the subject of the infinitive phrase, there is no need to repeat the noun.

1. *John* did not try something.
   John finished the job on time.
4. Something would take *us* three hours.
   We drive through the heart of the city.

In sentence 2, the infinitive phrase does *not* have as its subject a noun from the main clause; therefore, the subject of the infinitive phrase must be expressed.

2. Something is very difficult.
   A camel passes through the eye of a needle.

The transformation of this infinitive phrase may be expressed in a general way like this:

$$N_s + V + \text{remainder} \Rightarrow \text{for} + N_s + \text{to} + V + \text{remainder}$$

Sentences 3 and 5: In these sentences, the infinitive is a reduction of a wh-clause:

3. Sally doesn't know *something*.
   Sally mingles freely with people somehow.
       Wh-clause = how Sally mingles freely with people.
       Infinitive phrase = how to mingle freely with people.

    5. David always knows *something*.
       David does something in an emergency.
         Wh-clause = what David does in an emergency.
         Infinitive phrase = what to do in an emergency.

These reductions of the wh-clause are possible because the subject of the wh-clause repeats the subject of the main clause. Or we might explain this reduction by showing the subject of each infinitive phrase as a *some* word:

    3. *Someone* mingles freely with people somehow.
    5. *Someone* does something in an emergency.

Then the unnecessary *some* word is deleted to form the infinitive phrase.

THE PROCESS OF SUBORDINATION AND COORDINATION

Students have learned several different ways to combine sentences to form compound and complex sentences. Now they might be asked to combine pairs of sentences like these:

    1. Mr. Jones bought a new muffler for his car. The old one was rusted out.
    2. Niagara Falls is located right on the border between the United States and Canada. It is a great tourist attraction.
    3. Apparently something disturbed Bill. He had forgotten to lock the door to the lodge.

What factors led students to choose certain structures?

In example 1 there is a *causal* relationship—Mr. Jones bought the muffler *because* the old one was rusted out. Therefore, an adverbial clause of reason would seem to be the logical choice. Are there other possible choices?

Example 2, on the other hand, places two sentences together which have no logical connection, except that they both are providing information about Niagara Falls. A compound sentence is possible—"Niagara Falls is located right on the border between the United States and Canada, and it is a great tourist attraction"—but it is a weak construction because the two statements are not closely related in thought. When we note that both sentences are about Niagara Falls, we should realize that we can use a wh-clause to insert one sentence into the other. Here are two possibilities:

Niagara Falls, which is a great tourist attraction, is located right on the border between the United States and Canada.

Niagara Falls, which is located right on the border between the United States and Canada, is a great tourist attraction.

The choice of sentence depends upon what the writer wishes to emphasize. One of the sentences stresses the fact that Niagara Falls is a tourist attraction; the other stresses the location of Niagara Falls.

In example 3 we feel that the two sentences should be combined to get all the information into one sentence where it belongs, and to omit the unnecessary *something* from the first sentence. Obviously, the most natural procedure is to make the second sentence a nominal clause and put it in as the subject of the first sentence. Here are three possibilities:

Apparently, (his) forgetting to lock the door to the lodge disturbed Bill.

Apparently, the fact that he had forgotten to lock the door to the lodge disturbed Bill.

Apparently, it disturbed Bill that he had forgotten to lock the door to the lodge.

The selection of the method of combining sentences is determined by (a) logical and (b) structural factors. The writer must decide what logical connection he wishes to make, and he must use the transforms which the structure of the sentence makes available to him. It is important that he know which transforms are available to him so he can write with the greatest fluency and precision.

Exercise

For each of the following pairs of sentences, the student should think about the logical and structural possibilities for combining them into one compound or complex sentence. Then he should write what he considers to be the best possible sentence.

> Example: The water was still very cold.
> The children did not go swimming.
> Reasons for choice of structure: The first sentence states *why* the second sentence is true.
> Final sentence: Because the water was still very cold, the children did not go swimming.

1. We went to visit the Bryants.
   They were living in Baltimore then.
   Reasons for choice of structure:
   Final sentence:
2. Sam kept packing more baggage into the trunk of the car.
   The rear axle was nearly touching the ground.
   Reasons for choice of structure:
   Final sentence:
3. Harry wondered about something.
   How was he going to pay for the corsage and tickets?
   Reasons for choice of structure:
   Final sentence:
4. Arthur Jones wants to go to Florida this winter.
   He wants to sit in the hot sun during January.
   Reasons for choice of structure:
   Final sentence:

COMBINING SENTENCES

Few of us are ever happy with the first draft of a composition, whether it is a casual letter or a formal theme or essay. In expressing our ideas, we put down thoughts as they occur in the first words that come to mind. If we pause to grope for exactly the right words and structures, we are likely to lose our train of thought. But, after the composition is completed, we are free to read it over to make improvements in organization of ideas and in word choice. While there are many factors to consider in proofreading and correcting, we shall concern ourselves now only with sentence structures.

Let us assume that a writer has written a series of short sentences in a brief passage in his composition. As he wrote the passage, he knew that the ideas were important and related to each other, but he did not want to interrupt his train of thought to cast the sentences into their final form. Now, in revising, he faces the need to rewrite the series of sentences into one sentence which will reveal the relationships between the sentences and will create one well-unified thought. What is going to be the basis for his revision? Although the form which his revision will take will depend upon a variety of interlocking factors, let us consider several factors separately.

First, he must choose the one sentence in the series which he wishes to use for the main clause, the one upon which the whole structure will be built. A common principle in composition is that the main idea is stated in the main clause. But how does a writer select the main idea? Sometimes the main idea will be obvious because of its comparative importance, as in this example:

> Shirley walked into the living room. She tripped over a huge lion. The lion was stretched out on the floor. The lion was taking a nap.

To most of us, the main idea—the most striking, predominant idea —would be that Shirley tripped over a huge lion. If we decide that the complex sentence should be constructed upon that particular sentence, we find that the complex sentence will take shape naturally:

> As Shirley walked into the living room, she tripped over a huge lion which was stretched out on the floor, taking a nap.

At other times, the main clause may be selected more because it provides a logical focus than because it is particularly important. For example:

> Professor Kerr ate his lunch. He read a fascinating article in the newspaper. He put salt into his coffee and sugar on his peas.

None of those statements is of striking importance. However, there seems to be a natural means of structuring those sentences by telling why the professor improperly seasoned his food, and apparently did not notice his mistake. We might use some such organization as this:

> Professor Kerr, who was reading a fascinating article in the newspaper while he ate his lunch, put salt into his coffee and sugar on his peas.

Exercise

In each of the following groups of sentences, the student should underline the sentence he wants to use as the main clause. Then he should write a complex sentence which includes all of the sentences.

1. The ocean liner pulled into its berth. A dozen government agents rushed aboard. They were looking for diamond smugglers.
2. Jim was packing his suitcase. He was getting ready to check out of the hotel. He looked out the window and saw a wall of fire.
3. The sun beat down. The sand reflected shimmering rays of heat. The prospector walked steadily on. He was heading for the next water hole.

Now students should examine the complex sentences which they have just written, enclose each transform in parentheses, and then write the name of the transform.

MORE ON COMBINING SENTENCES

When a writer wishes to have more than one main clause, he may write a compound sentence. Or he may write a compound-complex sentence, a sentence which is formed of multiple main clauses and at least one subordinate clause. For the following example, the student should be asked to decide how he would construct a compound or compound-complex sentence.

> The history class went to the museum. Mrs. Adams went shopping. She was the faculty supervisor. Mrs. Graham went to a movie. She was the driver of one of the cars.

There are three sentences which tell what three people (or groups) did. Which of the following compound-complex sentences best combines those actions?

1. The history class went to the museum, but Mrs. Adams, who was the faculty supervisor, went shopping, and Mrs. Graham, who was the driver of one of the cars, went to a movie.
2. When the history class went to a museum, Mrs. Adams, (who was) the faculty supervisor, went shopping, and Mrs. Graham, (who was) the driver of one of the cars, went to a movie.

In the following example, all three actions in the three sentences appear to be of about equal importance, with one action simply coming after the other.

The elephant carried the huge log several hundred yards. The elephant dropped it into the river. The current in the river carried it down to the saw mill.

For this group we might write a sentence like this:

The elephant carried the huge log several hundred yards and dropped it into the river, where the current carried it down to the saw mill.

The compound structure in this case is a compound *predicate* rather than a compound sentence. Why is this structure possible?

Exercise 2

The student should combine each of the following groups of sentences to form one good sentence. He should have at least one compound structure in each of his sentences.

1. John opened the door. The two dogs scampered in. The parakeet flew out.
2. The rain stopped. The clouds quickly disappeared. The sun shone brightly for the rest of the day.
3. Danny opened the door of his car. Sue walked loftily past him. She entered Henri's limousine.

COMPOUND STRUCTURES

When we use compound elements in a sentence, we are, in effect, combining two sentences which have certain structures in common. For example, the two sentences

John lives on Elm Street.
Mary lives on Elm Street.

may be combined into one sentence because they both have the same predicate. We may write, "John and Mary live on Elm Street." Any grammatical units may become parts of compound elements.

Predicates: John *sat in the station* and *waited for his train.*
Noun Phrases: The lumberjacks cut down *all the pines* and *half of the spruces.*
Auxiliaries: Each voter *can* and *should* support his political party.
Prepositions: Mr. Withers walks *up, down,* and *across* the street all day long.
Adverbial clauses: *After Tom left home,* but *before he arrived at school,* he lost his lunch money.
Nominal clauses: Sam didn't know *what the raccoon would eat* or *where he was going to put the cage.*

The two or more sub-parts which make up a compound structure are called *parallel* structures. Each of the sub-parts of the compound structure serves the same grammatical *function;* it is natural, therefore, that we expect each of the sub-parts to have the same grammatical *form.* Thus a compound phrase like this would not be acceptable:

Henry loves to fish. ⎫
Henry loves swimming. ⎬ Henry loves to fish and swimming.
                      ⎭

Both sub-parts should be either infinitives or gerunds, as in these sentences:

Henry loves *to fish* and *(to) swim.*
Henry loves *fishing* and *swimming.*

Exercise

In each group of sentences below, the student should underline the structures which may be made compound. Then he should write one sentence, making certain that all sub-parts of a compound structure are parallel in both function and form.

Example: Dick strolled *through the woods.*
Dick strolled *across the meadow.*
Dick strolled through the woods and across the meadow.

1. Huck searched for snakes in the meadow.
   Huck searched for frogs in the old mill pond.
2. John was responsible for collecting the eggs.
   His little sister Katy was responsible for collecting the eggs.
3. It is important that Sheldon complete high school.
   It is important for Sheldon to go to college.
4. Mr. Henderson builds miniature trains to make a living.
   Mr. Henderson builds miniature trains as a hobby.

In sentences 3 and 4, did the student change the structure of one of the sub-parts of the compound structure to keep consistent grammatical forms?

What change did he make in the verb in sentence 2? Why was the change necessary?

PUNCTUATION

The writing of compound structures often requires the careful use of punctuation, which should present no problems if the student is familiar with the structures involved. Punctuation simply involves the use of symbols to guide the reader through a sentence with the least confusion possible.

Using commas, the student should punctuate the following sentences so that the structure of each sentence will be immediately clear to the reader.

1. Dad saw Jim Harry James and Sam at the game last night.
2. The little boy wandered into the house looked through all the rooms and finally fell asleep on the living-room floor.

3. For two hours John talked to his girl and then his father asked him to hang up.
4. Jody stuffed the dates Cathy cracked the walnuts and Suzy made the fudge.

Why did the student use each comma?

Since Harry James is a well-known band leader—but Harry and James also are common first names—why may punctuation be important in making sentence 1 completely clear?

How might sentence 3 be misread if the comma were omitted?

Those sentences illustrate a basic use of comma punctuation: to prevent confusion, a writer often places a comma between the sub-parts in a parallel series. We may, in general, follow these specific guidelines: (a) A comma occurs between each of the main clauses in a compound sentence; (b) A comma occurs between each of the sub-parts in a parallel series when there are more than two sub-parts.

Exercise

The student should rewrite each of the following groups of sentences as one sentence, using a compound structure in each sentence. He should punctuate each sentence carefully.

1. Skeeter rented a boat at the pier. He rowed across the river. He caught twelve bullfrogs.
2. For five days a week Rusty is just a regular college boy.
   On Saturday he is the football coach for a sandlot team.
   On Sunday he is the preacher in a country church.
3. Diana thinks that her oldest brother is a great athlete.
   Diana thinks that her younger brother is the best student in the whole school.
   Diana thinks that she is insignificant compared to them.
4. Henry leads an exciting life.
   Henry has visited Europe several times.
   Henry often goes on hunting trips to Alaska.
   Henry has just returned from a tour of South America.

PARALLELISM

The use of parallel structures, a desirable goal in writing, is very closely related to the matter of combining two or more sentences into one by making use of compound elements. The teacher may wish to give students an example like the one below and then ask questions like those that follow the example.

The man owned a dog.   He owned a turtle.

What is the structure of those two sentences? (Each is a pattern 3 sentence: $NP_s + VP_{tr} + NP_o$.) To what extent is the wording of each identical? (Each begins with "The man [or He] owned _____." Only the wording of the objects differs.) How do we combine these sentences? (The identically worded parts of each sentence need to be used just once.) Example:

The man owned $+ NP_o$ and NP_o.   (or)
The man owned *a dog and a turtle.*

The teacher should emphasize that the elements joined by the conjunction are *both the same kind of grammatical structure.* Not only do we now have a compound object but we have one whose elements employ parallel structure—that is, both objects are noun phrases (as indeed they must be, following a transitive verb). Although the example above may seem obvious, we find that some students have a better chance of grasping the idea of identical structures when the illustration is very simple.

Exercise

The student should study each sentence below and underline the elements which show parallel structure. In each case, he should tell the form and function of the parallel structures.

Example: a. *A fat dog* and *the young girl*
$\qquad NP_s \qquad\qquad NP_s$
stood near the corner.
b. The boy *reads* and *writes* every day.
$\qquad VP_{intr} \qquad VP_{intr}$

1. Three apples and some oranges are in the basket.
2. We all brought a few books and our pencils.
3. Our star player slipped and fell.
4. The students seemed calm, serious, and eager.
5. The frightened rabbits scampered through the bushes and into the woods.
6. After dawn but before breakfast, Joe worked out in the gym.
7. An intelligent and studious co-ed won the prize.
8. The class has neither read a book nor written a paper.
9. A fat, sleek, furry squirrel dashed up the tree.
10. A flying saucer sailed over the house, around the trees, and behind the water tower.

Do parallel structures have to be joined by *and*? What punctuation is used with some sets of parallel structures? What word can replace the punctuation? When do we use punctuation instead of a conjunction?

MORE COMPLEX STRUCTURES

The use of parallelism in structuring more complex sentence parts is difficult for most people. Usually lack of parallelism does not obscure meaning. However, in longer sentences, parallel structures can be helpful to the reader since they underscore the logical relationship between sentence parts. Indeed, skillful writers employ parallelism from one sentence to the next and even from one paragraph to the next to provide both a sense of direction and of unity.

The exercises which follow give the student practice in understanding and developing sentences involving parallel structures, but it will take appropriate emphasis in the student's own composition work to reinforce this notion effectively.

Exercise

The student should combine each set of sentences into a single sentence using as few words as possible. Then he should underline the elements which show parallel structure.

1. My briefcase looks old.   My briefcase looks worn.
2. My briefcase is old.   My book is old.
3. My briefcase is old.   My book is old.   My pencil is old.
4. That car seems new.   That car runs well.
5. Uncle Ted works rapidly.   Uncle Ted works easily.
6. Ed's clothes are scattered around the room.   Ed's clothes are scattered along the hall.

Did the student find it necessary to change the form of the verb in any of the sets? Which ones? Why? Did he find any set (or sets) which caused him to use the word *and* too often? Which? How can he avoid using *and*?

COMBINING DIFFERENT STRUCTURES

We can combine elements other than the form-word phrases to construct just one sentence employing parallel structures, as in these sentences:

1. My aunt went home because the snow had stopped and because she had to fix supper.
2. The boy who sells papers and who lost his bicycle can't make his deliveries.

We can break each of those sentences into two or more simpler sentences. For example:

My aunt went home *for some reasons.*
The snow had stopped. (first reason)
She had to fix supper. (second reason)

Since the second and third sentences give reasons for the aunt's leaving, they can be transformed into the adverbial clauses, "because the snow had stopped," and "because she had to fix supper."

If sentence 2 were broken into its component sentences, it would look like this:

The boy can't make his deliveries.
The boy sells papers.
The boy lost his bicycle.

The repetition of the noun-phrase indicates that we can apply the wh-transformation to the second and third sentences to form the complex sentence as shown in sentence 2.

Here is another set of sentences:

> Paul ran home again.   He had to get a hat.   He had to get the tickets.

What are the possibilities of combining those sentences? We could, of course, use adverbial clauses, as in this sentence:

> 3. Paul ran home again because he had to get a hat and because he had to get the tickets.

But such a combination is wordy. It is much simpler to use this reduced infinitive-phrase form of the adverbial clause:

> 4. Paul ran home again to get a hat and to get the tickets.

In sentence 3 we repeated the word *because* and in sentence 4 we repeated the infinitive *to get*. Is it necessary to do so? To what extent is repetition necessary in building parallel structures? Does the length of the structure have anything to do with it? For example:

> The airliner landed.   It was rainy.   It was foggy.

There we have two relatively short sentences that we may use as the basis for parallel structures. Which of the following combinations seems to be better?

> The airliner landed *because of rain* and *because of fog*.
> The airliner landed *because of rain* and *fog*.

Which of the following sentences is the best? Why?

> George likes to swim.   He likes to fish.   He likes to hunt.
> George likes to swim, to fish, and to hunt.
> George likes to swim, fish, and hunt.

Exercise 1

Each set of sentences below can be combined into one sentence containing parallel structures. The student should tell which sentence (or sentences) in each set can be used to form parallel structures. He should also tell what form each can be made into (some sentences may take more than one form). Then he should combine each set in the clearest, least wordy single sentence that he can.

Examples:

    a. The fish amaze me. (Use as the main clause.)
       They are very small. (Use as an adjectival phrase.)
       They are blue. (Use as an adjectival phrase.)
       They are hungry. (Use as an adjectival phrase.)
       These very small, blue, hungry fish amaze me.

    b. This morning John called his mother. (Use as the main clause.)
       He wanted to learn his father's middle name. (Use as an adverbial clause: "because he wanted to learn . . . ," or reduce to an infinitive phrase: "to learn . . .")
       He had to ask for lunch money. (Use as an adverbial clause or reduce to an infinitive phrase.)
       This morning John called his mother to learn his father's middle name and to ask for lunch money.

1. The boy's father treasured his arrowheads.
   He treasured his rock collection.
   He treasured his old swords.

2. Finally Mr. Silver became very disgusted.
   He had waited all night for the train.
   No one had brought his lunch.
   He hadn't had a chance to wash.

3. A young man bought a ticket to Rio.
   The young man was acting strangely.
   He was wearing dark glasses.

4. Some things raised Miss Tone's spirits.
   The sun was shining.
   The birds were singing.
   The flowers were blooming.

5. You have made your bed sometime.
   You have swept the floor sometime.
   Then you may go swimming.

Exercise 2

Below are some sentences containing compound elements which are *not* in parallel form. The student should (a) underline the compound elements as they stand now and tell the form and function of each, and (b) rewrite each sentence so that the compound elements *are* in parallel form. (There may be more than one way of rewriting.)

Example:

My pal Sam likes *hunting* and *to fish*. (not parallel)
          gerund/obj   infinitive/obj

My pal Sam likes hunt*ing* and fish*ing*. (*-ing* forms parallel)
(or)
My pal Sam likes *to hunt* and *to fish*. (infinitive forms parallel)

1. The professor works best in the morning and after the sun has set.
2. A stamp collector enjoys finding rare issues and to sell at a profit.
3. Because of his talent and because he is wealthy, Mr. Cox enjoys life.
4. Miss Prue came to school in spite of the bad weather and although she was sick.
5. A man running a gas station and who races cars should be able to have fun.

Exercise 3

The student should examine carefully an essay or short story, copying at least five examples of sentences which use parallel structures. Each example should show a *different* kind of parallel structure. The student should be prepared to tell the class the form and function of each set of parallel structures.

Exercise 4

The student should write at least five sentences, each containing a different kind of parallel structure. He should underline the parallel structures and tell their forms and functions.

Exercise 5

The student should examine one of his recent themes carefully, looking for as many examples of parallel structures as he can find.

He should rewrite five sets of sentences that can be combined so that they *do* contain parallel structures.

ADVERBIAL CLAUSES

Frequently a writer wishes to state a specific relationship between sentences rather than use a compound structure. To do so, he may choose from more than twenty-five *subordinators*. (The kinds of subordinators are considered in some detail in the eighth-grade program, and we looked at some examples in the grammar review section of the ninth-grade program.) To help students remember the subordinators, the teacher may have them fill the blanks in the sentences below with as many subordinators as they can.

> *Time* relationships: The fish were biting _____ the moon rose.
> *Place* relationships: Sandy stood _____ the parade would pass.
> *Manner* relationships: The professor leaned back in his chair _____ he had nothing else to do all day.
> *Reason* relationships: Tom was late _____ he had a flat tire.
> *Purpose* relationships: Carmen studied hard _____ she could get all A's.
> *Conditional* relationships: John will be considered for the position _____ he is in the Army Reserve.

A writer can be completely clear in stating a specific relationship between sentences if he chooses his subordinator with care. As we learned in grade eight, the combination of *subordinator* + *sentence* is an *adverbial clause,* whose function is expressed as a *some* element—*sometime, somewhere, somehow.*

An adverbial clause often is a movable unit; it can appear either at the beginning or the end of a sentence, or it can, at times, appear within a sentence. For example:

> Harold worked for a farmer *while he was on vacation.*
> *While he was on vacation,* Harold worked for a farmer.
> Harold, *while he was on vacation,* worked for a farmer.

Thus a writer may move adverbial clauses around to achieve clarity of statement and accuracy of fact. He may also move them for emphasis.

Exercise 1

The student should underline all of the subordinators in the
following passage.

> As soon as the agent from A.U.N.T. figured out the secret
> code of Starling, he dashed to the chief's office. He had to wait
> impatiently while the chief manipulated the dials of whirring
> computers. Finally, the chief, glancing up as if he were pro-
> voked by this interruption, demanded, "What is it now?"
> The agent coolly responded, "If you have time for such
> trivia, sir, I'd like to report that we can now monitor all of
> Starling's messages. I have come to you for instructions so that
> we can put Operation Z into action without delay."

The student should try to read the passage above with the subordinators omitted. What is lost when they are omitted? The student should note how the subordinators guide the reader from
sentence to sentence.

Exercise 2

The following passage does not contain any subordinators. The
student should read the passage, determine logical relationships
between sentences, and provide appropriate subordinators. He
may want to change the order of sentences by using introductory
adverbial clauses.

> The troop of Boy Scouts finally arrived at the camp site.
> They threw down their packs and sank to the ground. The
> scoutmaster was exhausted. He cheerfully called out, "Let's go,
> boys. Set up camp." The boys just groaned and did not move.
> Eddie Jones, one of the patrol leaders, staked out the patrol
> area. He wanted to set a good example. He built a fire to start
> lunch. The other scouts struggled to their feet. The camp area
> took shape quickly. Everyone did his assigned task.

PUNCTUATION

To keep sentence structures clear, a writer often must use commas to set off adverbial clauses so that the reader will know where
each clause begins and ends.

The teacher may put sentences like these on the chalkboard to show students how punctuation helps the reader to understand a sentence.

As I walked by the policeman was writing out a ticket.

Jim Wilson when he realized that he would have to cut the grass himself stopped complaining about the appearance of the lawn.

Stan will help you with the campaign if you ask him.

Those three sentences show the three possible situations for adverbial clauses—an introductory clause, a clause within another sentence, and a clause at the end of another sentence. In which of the three sentences are commas needed to make the structure completely clear? In which sentence is the comma optional?

Exercise

Have each student cut from a magazine article a paragraph which is 150 to 200 words long. Then have the student circle all coordinating conjunctions and all subordinators in his paragraph, and look carefully at those joining words. What kinds of compound structures appear? Which coordinating conjunctions occur most commonly? Which subordinators are used? Which adverbial functions occur most often (e.g., time, manner, condition, and so on)?

The teacher may have students compile statistics from their separate paragraphs to get a sampling of the structures used by today's writers. Students should also examine the punctuation in the paragraphs.

Students may be asked to examine their own themes to see how their use of compound structures and adverbial clauses correlates with that of the professional writers. Are any structures being overlooked by students?

ADJECTIVAL CLAUSES

The adjectival clause was explained in considerable detail in the eighth-grade grammar program, and it was reviewed in the introductory exercises of the ninth-grade program. Thus we assume a good general understanding of adjectival clauses as we review a few problems which arise in connection with these clauses.

We begin with an exercise aimed at giving the student practice in separating complex sentences into their sub-sentences and in answering questions about form and function.

Exercise 1

The student should study each complex sentence given below and then follow the instructions at the end of the exercise. The student should note particularly that each sentence contains an adjectival clause with either *who* or *whom* as its wh-word.

1. We met the girl who will be our baby sitter.
2. Some of the men who had been sitting nearby carried the winner on their shoulders.
3. Each student who has a perfect paper should feel proud.
4. Pay no attention to those people who complain all the time.
5. We all liked the policeman who directed traffic near our school.
6. My parents like the girl whom I met at the dance.
7. You may vote for the candidate whom you prefer.
8. The man whom you invited to dinner should be arriving.
9. At the airport the crowd missed the singer whom the police had secretly whisked away an hour earlier.
10. Do not criticize any of these boys whom the teacher failed.

a. Separate sentences 1 through 5 into their sub-sentences.
b. Underline the sub-sentences which appear as adjectival clauses in the complex sentences. Then circle the element which is replaced by a wh-word in the adjectival clause.
c. What is the *form* of each circled element? (noun phrase)
d. What is the *function* of each circled element? (subject)
e. What is the wh-word that replaces each circled noun phrase?
f. Separate sentences 6 through 10 into their sub-sentences.
g. Underline the sub-sentences which appear as adjectival clauses in the complex sentences. Then circle the element which is replaced by the wh-word in the adjectival clause.

h. What is the *form* of each circled element? (noun phrase)
i. What is the *function* of each circled element? (object)
j. What is the wh-word that replaces each circled noun phrase?
k. What conclusion can you draw about when to use *who* and when to use *whom*?

Exercise 2

Given below are groups of sentences that can be combined into one complex sentence containing an adjectival clause. The student is asked to use the second sentence in each set to form the adjectival clause, and to tell why he chose *who* or *whom* in each case.

1. Do you like the boy?   The boy has a new car.
2. The postman lives down the street.   The postman delivers our mail.
3. Here comes the messenger. We called the messenger an hour ago.
4. Those West Point cadets look handsome.   The cadets are wearing their dress uniforms.
5. Try not to make fun of the actors.   You don't like the actors.
6. The television star gives her goose-pimples.   The star sings through his nose.
7. We wrote a letter to an author.   We hadn't met the author.
8. The badmen didn't watch the sheriff.   They had knocked the sheriff off the cliff.

Exercise 3

The student should study each complex sentence below and then follow the directions below the sentences. As he studies the sentences, he should note that each contains an adjectival clause with *whom* as its wh-word.

1. Here is the girl whom I've written a story about.
2. Colonel Johns is the man whom I served under during the war.
3. The king is a man whom we must bow down to.
4. These spies are men whom we must act carefully with.

5. During the war Winston Churchill was a prime minister whom the people put much faith in.

   a. Underline each adjectival clause. Write each adjectival clause as a complete sentence.

   b. When you rewrote the adjectival clauses as sentences, were you able merely to replace *whom* with a noun phrase without changing the order of the words? For instance, in the first sentence if we merely replaced *whom* with *the girl,* we would have "The girl I've written a story about." We must change the order of the words to, "I've written a story about the girl."

   c. In each adjectival clause which is rewritten as a sentence, what kind of word precedes the noun phrase that replaces *whom?* (preposition)

   d. What do we call the function of a noun phrase following a preposition? (object of preposition)

   e. What conclusion can you draw about using *who* or *whom* to replace the object of a preposition?

   f. Look again at the adjectival clause in the first sentence: "whom I've written a story about." Written as a complete sentence, it becomes, "I've written a story about the girl." What are the steps we take to turn this sentence into an adjectival clause?

      Step 1: *The girl* is an element repeated from the first sentence. Therefore we replace it with a wh-word: I've written a story about *whom.*

      Step 2: Can we use this word-group as it now stands as an adjectival clause? No, we must move *whom* to the beginning of the clause, to read, "*whom* I have written a story about."

Is it possible to put the words in any other order? Look at the following sentences:

1. Here is the girl about whom I've written a story.
   Here is the girl whom I've written a story about.
2. Colonel Johns is the man under whom I served during the war.

Colonel Johns is the man whom I served under during the war.

3. Jones found a box into which we can put our skates.
Jones found a box which we can put our skates into.

4. The king is a man before whom we must bow down.
The king is a man whom we must bow down before.

5. Give me a hammer with which I can crack this walnut.
Give me a hammer which I can crack this walnut with.

From these examples, what general statement can you make about the placement of the preposition and the wh-term when the wh-term is the object of a preposition?

Exercise 4

In the following sentences, the student should underline all the nouns which are followed by adjectival clauses.

1. The boy who sits there always gets good grades.
2. All the men who came early will be sure to leave early.
3. The book that I'm reading has very few pictures.
4. He never saw the movie that he talks about so much.
5. Lend me the book which Miss Smith recommended.
6. This is the folder from which the papers came.
7. There is the dog that usually barks at the mailman.
8. The dog which Gallagher bought couldn't scare anyone.
9. There are the soldiers that I told you about.
10. I have found the article about which you were speaking.

    a. Divide a piece of paper into two columns. Head one column "human" and the other "non-human." Put each noun you underlined into one column or the other, depending on the nature of the noun.

    b. After each noun write the wh-word (or its equivalent) from the adjectival clause which follows the noun.

    c. What conclusions can you come to about the choice of wh-word (or its equivalent) if the noun refers to a human being? If the noun refers to a non-human being or object?

d. In which of the sentences can *that* be substituted for the wh-word? What is the special feature of the phrase in which the wh-word occurs when it *cannot* be replaced by *that*?

Are there any other wh-words that we can use in forming adjectival clauses? Let us look at the following sets of sentences.

1. Cap'n John searched for a place.
   The company could cultivate oysters somewhere.
2. The old-timers couldn't remember a time.
   So many tourists flocked to Fort Despair sometime.
3. Miss Pross told Jerry the reason.
   Everyone should protect her Ladybird for some reason.

We can turn the second sentence in each set into an adjectival clause. Note the repetition of the nouns *place, time,* and *reason* in the *some* elements in the second sentences. Such repetition indicates that a wh-word replacement is called for:

where the company could cultivate oysters
when so many tourists flocked to Fort Despair
why everyone should protect her Ladybird

If we make the wh-transform a part of the first sentence in each group, we have to put it immediately after the nouns *place, time,* and *reason.* An adverbial clause can be moved about in a sentence, but adjectival clauses cannot be moved. The sentences must read:

Cap'n John searched for a place where the company could cultivate oysters.

The old-timers couldn't remember a time when so many tourists flocked to Fort Despair.

Miss Pross told Jerry the reason why everyone should protect her Ladybird.

PUNCTUATION OF ADJECTIVAL CLAUSES

When we write a sentence containing an adjectival clause, we are faced with a problem of punctuation. Do we set the clause off with commas, or don't we? By examining a few sentences, we can discover some general principles.

1. A man who likes ice cream may get fat.
2. Some girl who was at the party lost her coat.
3. Few people who have money advertise their wealth.
4. Not many dogs that win prizes are mutts.
5. Not all girls who are beautiful win beauty contests.
6. Bill Smith, who mows my lawn during the summer, owns a better car than I do.
7. My oldest uncle, whom we all respect, dislikes saxophone players.
8. We invited Estelle, whose brother is a hockey player, to the junior prom.

Does there seem to be a consistent pattern to the use of commas in the sentences above? Look at the noun phrases which precede the clauses. Which of the noun phrases refer to *specific* things or people? Which refer to *nonspecific* things or people? Does that offer us an indication as to when to use commas and when not to? Can we say that when the noun phrase refers to *one particular* person or thing that the adjectival clause is set off with commas?

Exercise 1

There is an adjectival clause in each sentence or group of sentences below. Sometimes the clause is set off from the rest of the sentence by commas; other times it is not. The student should study each set of sentences and answer the questions that follow.

1. A book that tells about spies is exciting.
2. *Confidential Agent,* which tells about spies, is exciting.
3. The baby who cried all night is now fast asleep.
4. Mrs. Smith's baby, who cried all night, is now fast asleep.
5. We watched the baby and the little boy. The baby, who had cried all night, was now fast asleep.

    a. Why are sentences 1 and 2 punctuated differently?
    b. Why are sentences 3 and 4 punctuated differently?
    c. Why are commas used in the second sentence of 5?

There are two labels commonly used to distinguish between the adjectival clauses which are set off by commas and those which are not set off by commas.

  a. A *restrictive* clause is not set off by commas. The restrictive clause is important in making a nonspecific noun more specific. Look at the sentences above which are not set off by commas to see this relationship between the noun and the adjectival clause which follows the noun.

  b. A *nonrestrictive* clause is set off by commas. The nonrestrictive clause follows a noun which is already specific. Look at the sentences above which are set off by commas to see this relationship between the noun and the adjectival clause.

What do the words "restrictive" and "nonrestrictive" mean? Why are these logical labels for the clauses?

Exercise 2

The student should write each set of sentences as one complex sentence containing one or more adjectival clauses. In each set, he should use the first sentence as the main clause, and he should punctuate the sentences very carefully.

  1. The plan does not look very practical.
     Lt. Greene suggested the plan.
  2. My uncle works in Farmington.
     Farmington is a shoe-manufacturing town.
  3. The ocean helps to buoy up a swimmer.
     The ocean contains a heavy concentration of salt.
  4. That green chair in the corner is the most comfortable chair.
     You repaired that green chair in the corner last week.
     I have never sat in the most comfortable chair.
  5. All of the roofs can be repaired by the carpenters.
     All of the roofs have been damaged by the hail.
     The carpenters were flown in from Jersey City.

NOUN CLAUSES

As we observed early in our study of grammar, the sub-parts of basic sentences are form-word phrases—noun phrases, verb phrases, and adjective phrases. However, there are times when the concept we want to express as a sub-part of a sentence—for example, as a subject or an object—cannot be expressed in a phrase. Then we use the transform of a sentence in place of the phrase, as the italicized transforms in these sentences illustrate.

1. John suddenly realized *that the room was filling with smoke.*
2. The trouble is *that you forgot to fill the gas tank.*
3. Mike did not tell us *why he was afraid of the dogs.*
4. The farmer won't appreciate *your tearing apart his stone wall.*
5. *Rowing that boat against the wind* was very difficult.

Those transforms are used as nouns and are called *nominal* transforms. As sub-parts of basic-sentence structures, nominal transforms are required elements. (Adverbial and adjectival transforms are, in general, optional sentence elements.)

Sentences 1 and 2 illustrate the *that-clause* transform, sentence 3 illustrates the *wh-clause* transform, and sentences 4 and 5 illustrate the *gerund* transform. These were all considered in the eighth-grade course and reviewed early in the ninth grade. In the ninth-grade review we also examined the following *infinitive* transforms:

6. Sam doesn't know *how to drive a truck.*
7. It is natural *for a dog to swim.*
8. *To lift such a heavy weight* took great strength.

These steps produced each of those transforms:

6. Sam (*or* someone) drives a truck somehow
   ⇒ how Sam (or someone) drives a truck (wh-clause)
   ⇒ how to drive a truck
7. A dog swims ⇒ for a dog to swim
8. Someone lifts such a heavy weight
   ⇒ for someone to lift such a heavy weight
   ⇒ to lift such a heavy weight

Sentences 6 and 8 drop the subject because the subject does not provide any essential information; either it is a *some* element or it repeats the subject which has already been stated. In sentence 7, which illustrates a very common structure, the subject is needed.

The sentence does not begin with the infinitive phrase (which is functioning as subject), though such a structure is possible.

For a dog to swim is natural.

Instead, the sentence begins with *it*, and the infinitive phrase comes at the end of the sentence. There is a strong tendency for English sentences to place nominal transforms at the end of a sentence, even when they occur as subjects. Observe these examples:

9. It is inconvenient *to keep all of those papers on the dining room table.*
10. It is very important *for athletes to keep in good condition at all times.*
11. It is evident *that the students did not prepare their lessons.*
12. It is not known *how the swallows are able to return on the same date each year.*

In the following example, the *it* replaces a nominal transform which is not functioning as subject. What *is* the function of the transform?

13. The wind makes *it* very easy *to fly a kite today.*

Which of the sentences 9 through 13 can be rewritten by dropping out *it* and by placing the nominal transform in its regular position in the sentence pattern?

Exercise 1

The student should underline the gerund and infinitive phrases in the following sentences. Then the student should label the function of each underlined phrase. Finally, he should write the sentences from which the phrase reductions were formed.

1. Harold did not want to play quarterback.
2. Study hall is a good place for sleeping.
3. Sally has finally learned how to swim the backstroke.
4. Very few students are good at budgeting their time effectively.
5. It was easy for Fred to change the tire.

6. Mr. Jones pretended that he did not want to see the children.
7. Chopping down the tree took several hours.
8. It is not known how long the balloon will remain inflated.
9. Tim's job is to see that no one enters the clubhouse.
10. Not knowing what to expect of Ethel makes me uneasy.

Exercise 2

The student should write ten sentences, each containing a nominal transform. He should underscore each nominal transform and tell which function it serves.

SENTENCE COMPLETENESS

In this section we will treat the errors of sentence fragments, comma splices, and run-on sentences. Those errors are frequently treated more as matters of punctuation than of sentence structure. However, a student must have a knowledge of basic sentence structures, and must consciously apply that knowledge, if he is to avoid those errors.

THE SENTENCE FRAGMENT

Many fragments occur after a sentence of which they should have been a grammatical part. Fragments are usually recognizable as subordinate clauses or as reductions of subordinate clauses. If the student realizes that prose consists of basic and complex sentences, the latter of which employ subordinate clauses and their reductions as *parts*—and as parts only—of the whole sentence, then he will be less likely to write fragments. Realization, of course, is only a part of the problem. The habit of conscious application of grammatical principles is not easily come by.

Exercise 1

The student should study the word-groups below and answer the questions which follow.

1. Yesterday Bill Smith went to the lake. To go spear fishing.

2. Everyone in the club wore tuxedoes. Since the meeting was formal.

3. Chug-Chug Maloney came up with a clutch homer in the ninth. Winning the game.

4. Allan and Sue came to the dance with different dates. After telling everyone they were going steady.

5. Every night Sam fell into bed right after supper. Exhausted from unloading freight cars.

6. The customers were wet and unhappy. Having waited in the rain for the store to open.

7. Mr. Wilton came to class looking cross. Because someone had backed into his parked car.

8. Very soon Albert stopped raking. Since the wind had blown the leaves into the neighbor's yard.

9. Astrid managed to look satisfied. Although her cake didn't win first prize.

10. Honest John finally sold that car. A terrible oil-burner.

a. Which of the word-groups above are not sentences? Underline each one that is not and tell why it is not. What kind of grammatical structure is each?

b. Can each of the non-sentence word-groups be combined with the sentence standing before it? Must any of the wording be changed?

c. Why do you think people write fragments? Do you? Look back over some of the themes you have written. If you find any fragments, be sure to correct them.

d. Very frequently you will see fragments in newspaper and magazine advertising. Can you give reasons why advertising writers use fragments?

Exercise 2

We sometimes find fragments in what we call "good literature." Students should look carefully at a short story in one of their school texts—especially a story which uses quite a bit of dialogue. Do the people who are talking always speak in grammatically complete sentences? Students should copy a few lines of dialogue. Are all the word-groups that begin with a capital letter and end with a period grammatically complete sentences? Why, in a story, or in everyday conversation, do we feel that fragments are all right?

Students should now examine parts of stories where there is no dialogue. Do they find any fragments? What conclusions can they draw about the writers' use of fragments?

THE COMMA SPLICE

A very common error, the comma splice (also known as the "comma blunder" and "comma fault"), indicates that the writer does not recognize when he has reached the end of a sentence. He recognizes that there is a break, for he uses a comma between two sentences. Like the fragment, the comma splice depends for its cure upon the writer's conscious application of his knowledge of sentence structure.

Exercise

Students should study the word-groups below and answer the questions which follow.

1. John Jones is a fine athlete, he won three letters this year.
2. We saw the Earl of Cheshire yesterday, we were pleased when he waved to us.
3. After Bill saw his girl, he smiled at everyone, he was very happy.
4. The temperature rose twenty degrees, however, we kept our coats on.
5. John said that the test was hard, moreover, it was long.

a. In word-groups 1 and 2 above, write the form and function symbols above each of the form-word phrases. What basic-sentence patterns do you observe? What punctuation mark should follow a basic sentence?
b. In word-group 3 above, what kind of grammatical structure is "After Bill saw his girl"? Is it a complete sentence pattern or just part of a sentence pattern? Is it proper to put a comma after the word *girl*?
c. In word-group 3 above, what kind of grammatical structure is "he smiled at everyone"? What kind of grammatical

structure is "he was very happy"? Is it proper to put a comma after the word *everyone?*

d. In word-groups 4 and 5 above, give the form and function symbols for the grammatical structures before the first comma. Do you find recognizable sentence patterns? Is it proper to put commas after *degrees* and *hard* in groups 4 and 5, respectively?

e. In word-group 4 above, what kind of word is *however?* In word-group 5, what kind of word is *moreover?* What are the specific words that, together with a comma, can be used to join sentences? Do *however* and *moreover* belong to that group? (See pages 111-113.)

f. Properly punctuate each of the word-groups above.

g. Reread some of your themes. Do you find any places where you have separated two sentences with only a comma? Why do you think you made such an error?

THE RUN-ON SENTENCE

Another common error that resembles the comma-splice is the run-on sentence, which occurs largely because of the writer's haste and carelessness. To help the student develop his own awareness of the problem, he should examine the following sets of word-groups. The attack can be much the same as that used with the comma splice, with the student noting the occurrence of sentence patterns and reviewing appropriate punctuation.*

Exercise

The student should study the sets of word-groups below. He should give the form and function symbols for the form-word phrases, and draw a vertical line between the complete sentence patterns.

1. John's dog jumped over the fence he had just seen a cat.
2. Each of these sacks has been soaked in the rain all of the hamburgers are spoiled.
3. We wished the Scotland Yard detective would get here he seemed to be taking a long time.

*If teachers can teach their students to read run-on sentences properly, students will learn from the intonation patterns that punctuation is needed.

4. The newspaper was still soggy nevertheless the tramp tried to start a fire with it.
5. The commanding general was proud of his troops moreover they were proud of him.

STATEMENTS OF COMPARISON

Earlier in our study of grammar we saw that one of the distinctive features of the adjective is its ability to add the suffixes *-er* and *est* (or to be preceded by *more* and *most*). If an adjective appears in its simple form, we say it is in its *positive degree*. When it appears with the *-er* ending (or when it is preceded by *more*), we say it is in its *comparative degree*. When it appears with the *-est* ending (or when it is preceded by *most*), we say it is in the *superlative degree*.

In basic sentences like these, we can use the positive degree of adjectives:

The weather became *cool*.
The sunbather turned very *red*.

We do not usually use the comparative or superlative degrees of adjectives in basic sentences. For example:

Your mother's cake is sweeter.
This test seems easier.
Our house feels cooler.

As they stand, those statements pose such questions as "sweeter than what?" in the first sentence. We can phrase those sentences so they will not leave unanswered questions.

Your mother's cake is sweeter than my cake.
This test seems easier than the last test.
Our house feels cooler than your house.

We avoided unanswered questions by adding the structure word *than* and a noun phrase. We can do the same in sentences in which the comparative degrees of adjectives are formed by *more* + adjective, as in:

This shirt is more comfortable than the blue shirt.
That kettle is shinier than this kettle.

In the comparative sentences we've seen so far, there seems to be little need to fill out their structures to any greater length. Such sentences are elliptical (have words left out), and their complete forms look like this:

> Your mother's cake is sweeter than my cake is sweet.
> This test seems easier than the last test was easy.
> Our house feels cooler than your house feels cool.
> That shirt is more comfortable than the blue shirt is comfortable.
> That kettle seems shinier than this kettle seems shiny.

If the structure of one of those sentences was represented by symbols, it would look like this:

> Your mother's cake is sweeter than my cake is sweet.
> $\underline{NP_s + VP_{li} + Adj}$ + -er + than + $\underline{NP_s + VP_{li} + Adj}$

The underlined portions show that we have two sentences:

> Your mother's cake is sweet.   My cake is sweet.

But the relationship between them is undefined. Both cakes possess some degree of sweetness. We show that one is sweeter than the other by using the *-er* ending on the adjective and by using *than* to join the two sentences.

After examining a few examples of such comparative statements, students should be able to make conclusions like these:

a. A statement of comparison is the result of combining two sentences.

b. Each of the two sentences contains the same adjective.

c. Each sentence contains a noun referring to the same thing. The repeated adjective modifies those nouns. (Of course, different things can be compared, as in "John is taller than Henry.")

d. The two sentences may be combined by using the comparative form of the adjective in the first sentence and by using *than* as a conjunction.

Most students will react by suggesting that a statement like "Our house feels cooler than your house feels cool" is unnecessarily long. They are right, of course. Hardly anyone produces a sentence like that under normal circumstances. The question that students must answer, then, is, What governs how much of the second sentence must be included after *than?* One approach is to return to the basic-sentence form: "Our house feels cooler." Given no other context, each reader or listener is free to fill out the rest of the comparison as he chooses. Students may suggest such possibilities as:

> Our house feels cooler than it felt cool this morning.
> Our house feels cooler than the North Pole feels cool.
> Our house feels cooler after the rain than it felt cool before the rain.

Each student might complete the comparison in a different way and still no one might approach what the original speaker had in mind. After some experimentation, students should be able to reduce those sentences to these:

> Our house feels cooler than it did this morning. (Note the presence of *did.*)
> Our house feels cooler now than it did (it felt) this morning.
> Our house feels cooler than the North Pole.
> Our house feels cooler after the rain.

We can make other comparisons without always using the *-er* form of the adjective. Students can probably suggest sentences like these:

> These tennis balls are less bouncy than those (tennis balls are bouncy).
> His gloves are as dirty as my gloves (are dirty).

What differences do we see? In the sentence about tennis balls, the adjective *bouncy* is preceded by *less* instead of *more*, but the conjunction *than* remains. In the last sentence the adjective *dirty* is preceded by *as*; this time *than* does not appear; it has been replaced by another *as*. Comparisons, then, may be stated in terms of *less than, equal to,* or *greater than*, relationships.

We can also make comparisons by using the words *not so*, as in:

> These tennis balls are *not so* bouncy as those.

So far in dealing with statements of comparison, we have used only linking verbs. Other verbs can be used as well. The teacher might ask students to consider sentences like these:

> Boys eat more noisily than girls.
> Sam worked harder than Joe.
> We slept more soundly than they.

In those sentences we have intransitive verbs, and adverbials follow the intransitive verbs. To remind students of the structures of linking-verb and intransitive-verb sentences, the teacher might put these sentences and their symbolic representations on the chalkboard:

> Pies are sweeter than lemons.
> $NP_s + VP_{li} + Adj + than + N$
>
> Joe ran faster than Sam.
> $NP_s + VP_{intr} + Adv + than + N$

To assure themselves that students realize the difference between those structures, teachers may have students break those sentences into the two from which they are formed.

> Pies are sweet.   Lemons are sweet.

In those sentences we have the linking-verb pattern, with the adjective functioning as subject complement.

> Joe ran fast.   Sam ran fast.

And in those sentences we have the intransitive-verb pattern, with the verb followed by an adverbial. In those sentences we have the word *fast,* whose adjectival and adverbial forms are the same. In the case of

> Boys eat more noisily than girls.

we notice that the adverbial occurs in the adj + -ly form, and that it is preceded by *more.* By now it should be obvious to students that comparative statements involving adverbials are formed in much the same way as those involving adjectives.

Nouns, too, can enter into statements of comparison, as in:

> We caught *more flies* than they did.
> *More girls than boys* wear their hair long.

Good usage requires us to be careful when we involve nouns in comparisons. We use *more* with all nouns, regardless of kind:

more candy	more grass
more parrots	more apples
more sand	more men

With nouns representing things that we can conveniently count, we must use the plural form with *more*. However, to indicate a *less than* relationship, we use *fewer* with nouns representing countable items, but *less* with nouns representing things that exist in mass or abstract quantity.

fewer boys	less wheat
fewer cups	less love
fewer airplanes	less water

Also, careful usage requires us to use the comparative and superlative forms as follows:

Mine is the fast*er* car of the two.
Mine is the fast*est* car. (superlative to refer to more than two)
May the *better* man win. (comparative to indicate two men)
May the *best* man win. (superlative to indicate more than two)

PROBLEMS IN STATING COMPARISONS

Poor statements of comparison usually result from these errors:

a. Failure to make clear what is being compared with what. This year I'm happy to say that I'm healthier. (than whom? than when?)

b. Failure to include enough information to avoid ambiguity. Boys eat more than cats. (Boys eat more food than cats do? Boys include cats in their menus?)

c. Failure to include words required in comparative structures or words required by the logic of the statement.

   1. Joe's story is as short and more interesting than Bill's. (Should read: Joe's story is as short *as* and more interesting than Bill's.)

2. This playground is smaller than any in the city.
   (Should read: This playground is smaller than any *other* in the city.)

Exercise 1

The comparisons below are incorrectly stated. The student should tell what is wrong with each sentence, and he should write the comparison correctly.

1. Aunt Martha's coffee tastes better.
2. Joe threw the ball as far and more accurately than Bill.
3. We think that Ann likes Mary better.
4. Mr. Pottle has sat there as long if not longer than Mr. Havens.
5. Of the four players, Ed Smith is the taller.
6. Uriah Jones thinks better.
7. People eat more than oysters.
8. Your painting is the most colorful of the two.

Exercise 2

Each student should bring to class five samples of comparative statements used in advertising—either in newspapers or magazines or on television. The student should point out which are valid comparisons and which are not. For each one that is not, he should tell how the advertiser *wants* us to interpret the statement; then he should finish the statement in at least two different ways, but in ways not intended by the advertiser. Why do advertisers frequently give us incomplete comparisons such as the following?

More dentists recommend Brand X toothpaste.

The comparison is incomplete. The advertiser wants us to feel that the majority of *all* dentists recommend Brand X toothpaste. Possible completions are:

1. More dentists recommend Brand X than Brand Y.
   (A true statement even if only two dentists recommend Brand X and only one recommends Brand Y.)

2. More dentists than cab drivers recommend Brand X toothpaste.

DANGLING ELEMENTS

Leaving out words often results in poorly constructed sentences. The student needs to learn what he may leave out without danger of being misunderstood. To introduce students to the problem of dangling elements, the teacher may give them sentences like these and ask questions like those below the sentences.

1. Reading his book, the boy noticed a torn page.
2. Having finished dinner, Uncle Al folded his napkin.
3. After finishing dinner, Uncle Al folded his napkin.
4. Jumping up and down, Bob caught a glimpse of the parade.
5. Before turning on the shower, I closed the window.
6. Having looked for the dog in vain, the farmer chased the cows by himself.
7. To understand girls, a boy must be a genius.

a. In terms of structure, what do all of the above sentences have in common? (Each begins with an introductory element.)
b. Does each introductory element contain a verb form? (Yes. If the teacher wishes, he can ask that each be pointed out.)
c. Does each introductory element contain an NP_s for the verb form in the element? (No.)
d. What grammatical element directly follows the introductory element? (The NP_s of the main clause.)
e. Draw an arrow from the NP_s to the verb phrase which follows it. Now draw an arrow from the NP_s to the verb form in the introductory element. Example:

Reading his book, *the boy* noticed a torn page.
NP_s

f. Is it reasonable to expect the boy to be reading something? Is it reasonable for the boy to notice something? (Yes to both questions.)

Next we may have students examine sentences like these:

1. Eating a stack of pancakes, the dishwashing machine disturbed Ted.
2. To understand girls, many dates must be had with them.
3. After putting out the dog, a can of beans fell off the shelf.
4. Turning on the shower, the hot water scalded me.
5. Having found a policeman, the accident was reported.
6. Turning up the volume, Bill's guitar sounded better.

a. In terms of structure, what do all the sentences above have in common? (They begin with an introductory element.)
b. Does each introductory element contain a verb form? (Yes.)
c. Does each introductory element contain an NP_s to go with the verb form? (No.)
d. What grammatical element directly follows the introductory element? (NP_s of the main clause.)
e. Draw an arrow from the NP_s to the verb phrase of the main clause. Draw an arrow from the NP_s to the verb form in the introductory element. Example:

Eating a stack of pancakes, *the dishwashing machine*
                                                    NP_s
disturbed Ted.

f. Is it reasonable for a dishwashing machine to disturb someone? (Yes.)

   Is it reasonable for a dishwashing machine to be eating a stack of pancakes? (No.)

In this second series of questions, the answers to question number 6 should make apparent what we mean by the term "dangling element." Since the introductory element contains no NP_s to go with the verb form in the element, we intuitively expect the first noun phrase in the following main clause to tell us who or what is doing the action indicated in the introductory element. When the writer has been careless, as in the second series of sentences, the reader finds himself confronted with an illogical statement. If the student can rewrite that kind of complex sentence as its two underlying sub-sentences, he should be able to see more readily what is wrong with it.

Because we are primarily concerned that the student recognize dangling elements in his own writing, we should help him to realize that an ability to carry his knowledge of grammatical structure into the process of proofreading his paper can help him avoid errors in structure which lessen his effectiveness as a writer.

Let us review the source of the introductory elements we have seen in the preceding sentences. After students have isolated the main clause from the introductory element in each sentence, they should have the following main clauses:

> The dishwashing machine disturbed Ted.
> Many dates must be had with them.
> A can of beans fell off the shelf.
> The hot water scalded me.
> The accident was reported.
> Bill's guitar sounded better.

If the introductory element can be made into an adverbial clause to follow its respective main clause, then we can rewrite the introductory elements as adverbial clauses. Thus we find that in sentence 1 there is this adverbial possibility:

> The dishwashing machine disturbed Ted *sometime*.

If we make a substitution for *sometime* in the introductory element, we get

> while he was eating a stack of pancakes.

Now, if we ask the student to recall what he has learned about reduced adverbial clauses, he should tell us that an adverbial clause may be reduced when its subject phrase repeats the subject phrase of the main clause. (For restrictions as to *which* adverbial clauses may be reduced, see page 127 of the eighth-grade grammar.) Now if the student examines the main clause and adverbial clause in each instance above, he can see that the subject of the main clause is *not* repeated in the adverbial clause.

> *The dishwashing machine* disturbed Ted while *he* was eating a stack of pancakes.
> *Many dates* must be had with them if *boys* are to understand girls.

A can of beans fell off the shelf after *Tom* put out the dog.

The hot water scalded me as *I* turned on the shower.

The accident was reported after *the witness* had found a policeman.

Bill's guitar sounded better when *he* turned up the volume.

As they stand, the sentences above are grammatically sound, if not stylistically ideal. They can be rewritten with the adverbial clauses reduced to introductory elements in sentences like these:

Eating a stack of pancakes, Ted was disturbed by the dishwashing machine. (This sentence is grammatically sound, but note that the main clause has been put in passive form. Most authorities on writing agree that we should try to avoid passive forms, but perhaps it is best not to tamper with the adverbial clause in this case.)

To understand girls, boys must have many dates with them. (This sentence is grammatically sound, *and* by putting the main clause in active rather than passive form, we have improved the sentence stylistically.)

After putting out the dog, Tom heard a can of beans fall off the shelf. (This is an acceptable sentence, but note that we had to supply an NP_s and verb phrase for the main clause.)

Turning on the shower, I was scalded by the hot water. (Again notice that we are forced to use the passive form in the main clause.)

Having found a policeman, the witness reported the accident. (This is an acceptable sentence. It is an improvement because the main clause now occurs in active rather than passive form.)

Turning up the volume, Bill made his guitar sound better. (This sentence is acceptable. Note the change in NP_s in the main clause.)

Exercise 1

The sentences below contain reduced subordinate clauses in the introductory position. Some of the reductions are "danglers." Others are not. If the student thinks a sentence is correct as it stands, he should simply write *C* after its number on his paper. If a sentence needs correction, he should rewrite it, using the same introductory phrase as the original.

1. While shaving in the morning, the toothpaste fell on Tom's toe.
2. After running a full mile, Jerry found himself perspiring.
3. Having strolled down the avenue, the museum loomed before me.
4. To swim expertly, several years should be spent with a good coach.
5. Before trying on the new suit, the mirror had to be adjusted.
6. On entering the room for the first time, a large armchair met my gaze.
7. Sitting down to eat, Albert became conscious of the cat sitting across from him.
8. Totally wrecked in the smashup, Fred considered his car to be worthless.
9. Wrapped in old newspaper, George found a packet of dollar bills.
10. By always being first in line, my uncle usually got the best cut of roast beef.

a. Did you find that you couldn't avoid using the passive form for the main clause in some of the sentences you rewrote?
b. Can you draw any conclusions about the advisability, in some cases, of beginning a sentence with a reduced subordinate clause?

Exercise 2

For additional practice in avoiding "dangling" introductory elements, the student should follow the directions given after each sentence. If in rewriting the sentence he cannot avoid putting the main clause in passive form, he may, instead, make appropriate changes in the introductory element.

Example: A loud truck woke Jim up. Begin the sentence with
sleeping during lunch hour.

Sleeping during lunch hour, Jim was awakened by
a loud truck. (Here the main clause has to be put
in its passive form. To avoid the passive, we can
change the introductory element to read as follows:

While Jim was sleeping during lunch hour, a loud
truck woke him up.)

1. A motorcycle leaped the curb and smashed the front of the
   Bon-Ton Shoppe. Begin the sentence with *before going to
   lunch.*
2. A tall glass of lemonade tasted good. Begin the sentence
   with *after mowing the yard.*
3. The burglar-alarm went off accidentally. Begin the sentence with *while testing the bank's security procedures.*
4. The express bus to Toronto left without us. Begin the sentence with *having taken too long to eat lunch.*
5. All these convicts must be watched closely. Begin the sentence with *to prevent a mass escape.*

PROBLEMS OF AGREEMENT

Hardly anyone has trouble choosing the right form of the verb
in sentences like these:

The man (go, goes) home at noon.
Four goats (was, were) munching the grass.
Each player (bring, brings) his own uniform.
Bingo and Monopoly (is, are) my favorite games.

But problems begin to arise in situations like these:

(a) when the NP_s contains an "of" phrase, as in the following:

each *of the men*
four *of the goats*
every one *of the players*

(b) when the overall NP$_s$ is composed of sub-phrases so that a mixture of singular and plural nouns occurs before the verb phrase:

the sound of the machines in the streets
every one of the books of poems

(c) when one of the elements joined by a conjunction is plural:

either the man or the boys
neither the planes nor the ship
not only the books but also the pencil
the man or the boys

(d) when any of the constructions in (a), (b), and (c) is followed by an adjectival clause:

each of the men who . . .
every book of poems which . . .
either the man or the boys who . . .

Let us consider the problem of (a). An effective method of attack is to give the students a series of sentences containing subject noun-phrases which are obviously either singular or plural and then have the students rewrite the sentences so that they begin with various "of" phrases. In the new sentences they will have to determine whether the "of" phrase indicates singular or plural, thus determining the form of the verb.

Exercise 1

The student should rewrite each sentence below according to the directions following it. Then he should answer the questions at the end of the exercise.

1. The men are coming home. (begin with "All of")
2. The men are coming home. (begin with "One of")
3. The men are coming home. (begin with "Each of")
4. Those players begin to look tired. (begin with "Every one of")
5. That book seems damaged. (begin with "All the pages of")
6. These rooms rent for eight dollars. (begin with "Either of")

a. Did you find it necessary to change any of the verb forms in any of the sentences when you rewrote them? Which ones?

b. What conclusions can you draw about the effect of an "of" phrase in making the NP$_s$ singular or plural?

In the next exercise we find one or more modifying phrases as sub-parts of the NP$_s$, so that a mixture of nouns, both singular and plural, occurs before the verb phrase. If the writer is in a hurry, he may well use an improper verb form as a result.

Exercise 2

The student should rewrite each sentence below according to the directions following it. Then he should answer the questions at the end of the exercise.

1. A book is lying on the table. (After *book,* insert "containing our favorite poems and several short stories")
2. Each man hopes for help. (After *man,* insert "in the clutches of his enemies")
3. The sound bothers us. (After *sound,* insert "of many machines in the streets")
4. An Eskimo travels through the snow. (After *Eskimo,* insert "accompanied by his wife and sled dogs")
5. Each of the girls is supposed to sit on the platform. (After *girls,* insert "wearing a blue dress and carrying red roses")

a. When you rewrote the sentences above, did you find it necessary to change any of the verb forms? Tell why or why not.

b. What effect do modifying phrases have in changing the number (singular or plural) of a noun phrase?

c. Examine a few of your compositions. Have you made proper choices of singular and plural verb forms?

In the next exercise we are faced with the problem of choosing the proper verb form in the adjectival clause. The student should learn to see the adjectival clause in its full sentence form in order to see more clearly the proper verb form.

Exercise 3

The sentences below contain adjectival clauses. For each adjectival clause, the student is given a choice of verb forms. Before he chooses a verb form, he should write each adjectival clause as a full sentence; then he should circle the appropriate verb form.

1. John is the boy who (park, parks) cars at the stadium.
2. John is one of the boys who (park, parks) cars at the stadium.
3. Be sure to pick up every book of poems which (contain, contains) Robert Frost's "Fire and Ice."
4. General Howe is one of those old campaigners who (like, likes) to tell tales of past engagements with the enemy.
5. We wrote an article about the leader of the regiments that (has, have) been chosen for special duty.

a. In each sentence, which noun standing before the adjectival clause did you choose for the NP$_s$ in putting the adjectival clause in its full sentence form? Do you find that the principles governing singular and plural verbs in adjectival clauses are the same as for the sentences in the first two exercises in this section? What, if any, are the differences?
b. Did you find, in this exercise, any sentence (or sentences) in which you can justify the choice of *either* a singular or plural verb in the adjectival clause? Which? Why?

The next exercise requires us to choose the proper verb form when we have noun phrases connected by conjunctions. In this case, the solution lies primarily in the conventions agreed upon by careful users of the language. To get the students involved, the teacher may give them some sentences like these to consider:

1. Either the man or the boys (was, were) to clean the shop.
2. Either the men or the boy (was, were) to clean the shop.
3. We can tell that neither the planes nor the ship (is, are) in a position to spot the space capsule.
4. Not only a dog but also several cats (has, have) sneaked into the meat-locker.

Undoubtedly students will be divided in their opinions about the proper verb forms, with no reasonable consensus forthcoming. The teacher can go on to show each of the sentences above with the conventional verb form used. Very possibly, then, the students may see why most authorities have agreed to make the verb form agree with the noun phrase that is closest to the verb.

Cumulative Exercise

The student is asked to choose the singular or plural form of the verb in the sentences below. He should be ready to tell *why* he chose each verb form.

1. All of the boys (is, are) entered in the swimming race.
2. Either of those doors (lead, leads) to the locker room.
3. Each one of the houses (show, shows) signs of age.
4. Not only the prize-winner but also the runners-up (receive, receives) a scholarship.
5. Johnson seems to be one of those men who never (give, gives) up.
6. Alex may turn out to be the culprit who always (use, uses) all the hot water.
7. How can we be sure that neither the two cars nor the motorcycle (break, breaks) down during the parade?
8. All the teachers and the principal (agree, agrees) that this is the best team in years.
9. The captain will make sure that the squad of ushers that (seat, seats) the spectators most quickly (get, gets) a prize.
10. Make certain that you have notified each of the winners or their sponsor as to who (is, are) to appear at the banquet.

PRONOUN AGREEMENT

Before we consider the problem of pronoun agreement, it might be well to review with the students the notion that a pronoun is a kind of word which we use frequently to avoid repetition of a noun phrase. For example:

All the papers are here. *They* need to be sorted.

"They" refers back to "All the papers." The noun phrase that the pronoun refers back to is called the *antecedent* of the pronoun. Touched upon in the eighth-grade program, but not emphasized, is the fact that the personal pronouns in English take distinct forms according to their function as subject or subject-complement, as object, or as possessive.

Exercise

Both the pronouns and their antecedents have been italicized in the sentences below. The student is to tell the *function* of each italicized pronoun, to follow the directions at the end of the exercise, and to answer the questions at the end of the exercise.

1. *A girl* approached the window. *She* looked at the tree outside.
2. We looked at *the nearest man*. Then we spoke to *him*.
3. No one knew *the man at the door*. We turned *him* away.
4. *Jack's* coat lay on the floor. *His* hat was on the chair.
5. *Those autos* make too much noise. *They* should have new mufflers.
6. *Ted's mother* visited us. We gave *her* the guest room.
7. Look at *the tired horses*. Don't you feel sorry for *them*?
8. *The man* we saw in the hallway was *he* who had lectured at school.
9. *The actors* chosen for awards were *they* who turned in good performances.
10. *The person* whom you called to last night was *I*.

Now divide a piece of paper into three vertical columns. Head one column "subject or subject-complement," another "object," and the third, "possessive." Write each italicized pronoun from the sentences above under the appropriate column-headings. Arrange the pronouns so that the different forms of the same pronoun occur on the same line.

	Example:	*Subject or Subject-complement*	*Object*	*Possessive*
		he	him	his

a. In the example above, we see that the pronoun which refers to one male being has three different forms—*he, him,* and *his.* Do all personal pronouns have *three* different forms?

b. State a rule that tells, as briefly as possible, when to use each form of the personal pronoun.

THE POSSESSIVE PRONOUN

There is one more pronoun form—the second form of the possessive—which enables us to avoid needless repetition of the antecedent noun. For example:

The red book is your book.
The red book is yours.

In the first sentence we find that we have to repeat the word *book.* But in the second sentence the pronoun *yours* eliminates the need for repetition. One might begin a discussion with the students with this question: "How do we use words like *hers, yours,* and *theirs*? In what way will sentences using these words look different from sentences using *her, your,* and *their*?"

Exercise

The student should choose the proper forms of the pronouns in the sentences below. In making up his mind which form to use, he should decide whether the pronoun functions as subject, or subject-complement, or object.

1. Joel and (we, us) waited outside the principal's office.
2. Mr. Fry gave Tom and (I, me) a dollar each.
3. I was happy to see that the prize was for Ted and (I, me).
4. They seemed glad to have (we, us) boys at the party.
5. Never have we known a person as irritable as (she, her).
6. If it hadn't been for Bill and (they, them) in the cast, the play would have been very poor.

PROBLEMS OF AGREEMENT

Another problem of pronoun usage is similar to that of choosing the proper verb form when the NP_s contains both singular and plural elements. In the case of the pronoun, however, we must deal with more than just the NP$_s$, for the antecedent of a pronoun may occur in other than the subject position. If the student has become proficient at determining proper verb forms, he should not have much difficulty with pronoun forms.

Exercise

After the student has decided which pronoun he would use in the sentences below, he should give a reason for his choice.

1. Either of the players may put on (his, their) uniform.
2. Each girl who makes the trip should bring (her, their) own lunch.
3. All the senators at the meeting expect to have (his, their) plans approved.
4. Everyone who wants (his, their) picture taken must wear (his, their) good clothes.
5. Not one of the spectators who came in late was allowed to go to (his, their) regular seat.

AMBIGUITIES AND MISPLACED ELEMENTS

Ambiguous statements—those with two possible interpretations—result primarily from carelessness rather than from ignorance of the principles of grammatical structure. However, a student writer's consciousness of grammatical principles can help him avoid being misinterpreted. It is our purpose here to consider only those problems which occur most frequently in the writing of high school students.

The use of pronouns offers inexperienced writers a good chance to confuse their readers, particularly when the pronoun follows a part of the sentence in which two nouns occur, either of which could be a logical antecedent for the pronoun. For the most part such ambiguities should be obvious to the student who takes the time to look at, and think about, what he has written.

Exercise 1

The sentences below contain personal pronouns that have been used so carelessly that a reader cannot be sure just what the antecedents of the pronouns are. The student's job is to study each sentence and then rewrite it so that no ambiguity remains.

Example: John told the man that he ought to be careful.
Rewritten: John told the man to be careful.

1. My aunt Jo wrote to Sally that it was time for her to come home.
2. After Tom had talked to George, he was glad that he had won.
3. Mary scolded her little sister because she was short-tempered.
4. Mitch didn't want to race against Ed because he had a sore leg.
5. The colonel really didn't care for the sergeant even though he always greeted him cheerfully.
6. She'd rather wear the dress than the suit because it is easier to clean.

Exercise 2

Other ambiguous—or at least misleading—statements occur when the writer forgets to place modifying elements properly in the sentence. In the exercise below, the student is given an opportunity to study sentences that need rewriting for clarity.

The sentences below contain modifying elements placed so that the reader cannot tell just what the writer had in mind. The student should rewrite each sentence to make it as clear as possible.

1. The little boy lay watching a butterfly perched upon a dandelion in a red shirt.
2. Every day the girls saw some birds building nests on their way to work.
3. Munching oats in the barn, Ellis found the spotted horse.
4. The medieval artist painted a picture for the duke that is hanging in the museum today.

5. Lazily the sheriff leaned back, took off his hat, and studied the photograph with a smile.
6. Freshly baked in the oven, Mom gave us all some cookies.
7. Club members missed the performance of the singer who came late.
8. They told us after lunch the game would be played anyway.

Exercise 3

The student is asked to combine each set of sentences below into a single sentence without omitting ideas or changing the meanings. He should try to use as many different grammatical structures as he can.

1. The boys in the house ate all the sardines. The boys were Joe's buddies.
2. The cat in the window washed its paws. The cat belongs to Sheila.
3. A rusty suit of armor near the window caught my eye. The suit of armor was used in the fifteenth century.
4. Yesterday Allan discovered an envelope in his house. The envelope contained Confederate battle-plans. The envelope was wrinkled and brown.
5. An old chair lay in the corner. The chair was covered with dust. The chair had no legs.
6. Mr. Olson often told us about the cars he had raced in Europe. Mr. Olson had nothing else to do.

ON TEACHING BASIC SENTENCE PATTERNS TO SLOW-LEARNING STUDENTS IN GRADES SEVEN THROUGH ELEVEN

By
EDWARD B. JENKINSON
Coordinator for School English Language Arts and
Director of the Indiana University
English Curriculum Study Center

On Teaching Basic Sentence Patterns
to Slow-Learning Students
in Grades Seven Through Eleven

Like their more academically talented classmates, slow-learning students need to know how words work in sentences to achieve a satisfactory level of proficiency in speaking, writing, and reading the English language. In conversation, slow learners have little difficulty putting words together in acceptable syntactical patterns; instead, they experience more difficulties with usage and vocabulary than with syntax. But in writing they usually have problems with usage, syntax, spelling, vocabulary, and punctuation. Nevertheless, slow-learning students, like their more academically talented classmates, already know a great deal about language, and, as we indicated in the grammar for academically talented and average students, that intuitive knowledge of English presents one of the major difficulties in teaching or in studying grammar. (See page 2.)

In presenting fundamental concepts of syntax, a teacher of slow learners must be very careful lest he inadvertently talk down to students and lose their attention for the semester. In going over basic sentence patterns, the teacher of slow learners must remind students that he knows that they already know a great deal about their language and that he is giving them the opportunity to reinforce what they already know by expanding basic sentences. In other words, slow learners must feel, at all times, that they are contributing to class discussions and that they know something; they must also feel that they are discovering something new as class discussion proceeds from the familiar to the new.

This method of presenting the structures of English sentences builds on the familiar; it incorporates concepts of traditional, transformational, and structural grammarians, relying primarily on the terminology of traditional grammarians wherever terminology is deemed important enough to be stressed. Although this approach deals primarily with English syntax, attention is also given to attendant matters of capitalization, punctuation, usage, spelling, and semantics. No attempt has been made to divide the program into grade levels. It is impossible to determine how many steps in this sequence a slow learner can master in any given grade. Therefore, the sequence is divided into steps that are presented in an order that has proved workable for teachers experimenting with the program in pilot schools, and the teacher is encouraged to move from one step to the next only after the majority of the students in his classes have mastered the concept presented in the first step.

Although the starting point for this program is grade seven, teachers in grades eight, nine, or even ten may wish to start with the first step if they feel that students need it. Again, teachers are cautioned to make certain that slow learners understand that they are reviewing concepts that students probably already know, paricularly if the teacher begins with the very first part of this program. Otherwise, slow students may quit listening because they feel they are being insulted. This approach is based on a number of assumptions.

1. Slow learners can learn more about their language and can become more proficient in speaking and in writing if they construct their own sentences rather than fill in the blanks in workbook sentences or analyze sentences in grammar textbooks.

2. Terminology provides convenient handles by which to get hold of certain elements in the language or by which to grapple with certain concepts. However, terms should not be presented before slow learners have an opportunity to examine a number of the elements or concepts. For example, only after slow learners see what nouns are and how

they work in sentences should they be introduced to the term, noun.

3. Definitions should not be forced upon slow learners; instead, slow learners should arrive at their own definitions of elements in English sentences after they have carefully examined a number of the elements. If a slow learner learns the definition that a noun is a name of a person, place, or thing, it is unlikely that this definition will help him in his attempt to understand what a noun is and how it works in a sentence. That definition should be discarded in favor of a definition that the class and the teacher make after they have examined a number of nouns to see what they do in sentences, how they can be detected, and, finally, what they are. Such a definition would call attention to inflection, to the positions that nouns can take in sentences, and to the modification of nouns by other words or groups of words.

4. Slow learners can best remember the concepts presented if they keep their own notebooks, filling them with sample sentences and with definitions they arrive at themselves.

5. Although the conventions of capitalization, punctuation, and usage are not necessarily a part of structure, they are included in this approach since they are attendant matters that can be taught while the student is learning to construct sentences.

This essay explains one approach to teaching four basic sentence patterns to slow-learning students. The patterns are arranged in an order that, through classroom testing, we have learned works best for slow learners. After students have mastered the concepts presented here, they can continue their study of syntax by beginning with the section on adverbials in the approach to grammar for academically talented and average students. (See page 40.) But as the teacher covers that material, he should continue to have students build sentences as they do in the approach explained in this essay. An explanation of how to cover the material in the other approach is appended to the end of this essay.

Each step in this approach and in the one for academically talented and average students provides sufficient repetition of the concepts presented in preceding sections so that slow learners will have the necessary reinforcement needed to retain what they have learned. This reinforcement does not rely on needless repetition; instead, it takes the form of a planned review of concepts already presented as new concepts are introduced.

In sentence pattern one, and in each succeeding pattern, teachers are encouraged to select their own verbs and have students build sentences with those verbs. The verbs presented in this program and the illustrative sentences need not be followed in class presentations. The teacher will want to select different verbs and illustrative sentences that will be more meaningful to his class and that will stimulate participation.

Teachers experimenting with this approach learned that with some classes it was far better to introduce the first four basic sentence patterns briefly before concentrating on noun and verb expansion. Other teachers learned that with certain classes they could follow the program as it is presented here without having to introduce all four patterns within the first week or two of instruction. Teachers are encouraged to experiment to discover which method works best with their students.

(Note: This program is designed to help slow-learning students build better sentences of their own by applying the intuitive knowledge they have about syntax to various sentence structures. As we indicated above, terminology is not stressed in this program, nor are the rules for forming or transforming sentences. Therefore, we urge teachers not to give slow learners tests in which students are given the basic sentence pattern formulas and are asked to construct ten sentences of each type; neither should teachers quiz students on definitions or rules. Instead, we encourage teachers to assign the writing of short paragraphs and to commend students highly on their ability to use a variety of sentences in those paragraphs. Surely the teacher can give a student a grade for class participation and for improvement in his own writing rather than base a grade on a test that only confuses the student by encouraging him to memorize rules and definitions that are relatively meaningless to him.)

SENTENCE PATTERN ONE—
$N_S + V_{INTR}$

Without indicating that the verb he writes on the board is a third-person singular, present-tense form of an intransitive verb, the teacher writes on the chalkboard a group of words like this:

The _____ walks.

He asks students, "Who or what walks?" He encourages students to give complete responses, i.e., "The cat walks," not simply "cat"; and the teacher writes the students' complete responses on the chalkboard. He writes each response as a complete sentence so that students will always see complete sentences, not fragments, on the chalkboard. As a student responds, he should say the complete sentence and also write it in his notebook. Responses might include:

The cat walks.	The Russian walks.
The dog walks.	The man walks.
The boy walks.	The woman walks.
The girl walks.	The child walks.
The American walks.	The ox walks.

After students have constructed a number of sentences containing the verb *walks,* the teacher writes other third-person singular, present-tense forms of intransitive verbs on the chalkboard in frames like this:

The _____ sings.

The teacher records the students' responses on the chalkboard, and each student writes his own sentences, as well as other students' contributions, in his notebook. Some sample responses might be:

The _____ runs.	The _____ talks.	The _____ jumps.
The cat runs.	The boy talks.	The child jumps.
The dog runs.	The girl talks.	The fox jumps.
The horse runs.	The student talks.	The man jumps.
The woman runs.	The teacher talks.	The American jumps.

After students have filled the subject slots with a number of nouns, the teacher asks them what three things the words inserted in the slots have in common. Responses should indicate that all are names of classes of human beings and animals; all precede words like *walks, runs,* or *talks;* all can be preceded by the word *the.* (Note: Students should analyze the sentences written on the chalkboard and they should generalize only on the basis of how nouns are used in those sentences. Since names for things or ideas are not likely to be used in these simple sentences, no mention is made, at this time, of nouns also being names of *places, things, actions,* or *ideas.* If students should respond with sentences like "The stocking runs" or "The car runs," then they should also see that some words that can precede *runs* can also be names of things.)

The teacher should establish, by asking students for the answer, why we use the convention of capitalizing the word *the* when it appears at the beginning of a sentence. The teacher might also ask why the words *Russian* and *American* are capitalized if such words are included in student responses. (The teacher should not expect the answer that words like *American* and *Russian* are capitalized because they are proper nouns; if he does receive such an answer, he should make certain that everyone in class understands what a proper noun is. After he has established why certain nouns are capitalized, he may wish to have students substitute other proper nouns for the words that students have already put in the noun slots.)

At this point the teacher can ask students what we call words like *cat, dog, man, woman, Russian,* and *American.* At least one student should know the word *noun,* and from this point on the word *noun* can serve as a convenient label for words (a) that name human beings or animals (or things), (b) that can immediately follow a word like *the,* and (c) that can precede words like *walks, runs,* and *talks.*

In each of the illustrative sentences that were written on the chalkboard, the noun was preceded by the word *the.* Now the teacher should remove the word *the* and ask students what single word they can substitute for *the.* Sample responses might be:

A cat walks.	This child jumps.
An American walks.	That fox jumps.
Every teacher talks.	My dog runs.

Words like *a, an, the, every, this, that,* and *my* pattern with nouns, and they (except *this* and *that*) always function as noun markers or determiners. If students ask what such words are called, the teacher can tell them that they are noun markers or determiners. The word *determiner* is particularly useful since it is used as a label for those words that always signal that a noun is following. (A more complete treatment of determiners appears on page 218, but the teacher will probably want to stop discussing determiners at this stage and bring them up again when students fill slots with plural nouns.)

Before the teacher constructs sentence frames that require plural nouns, he should make certain that students understand (a) that words like *cat, dog, man,* and *woman* are names that we give to classes of animals or human beings, (b) that we call these words nouns, (c) that nouns are words that can be preceded by words like *a, an, the, every, this, that,* and *my,* and (d) that nouns can precede words like *walks, talks, runs,* and *jumps.* The teacher will also have students note that the first word in each of the sentences on the board is capitalized and that the sentence ends with a period.

Students are now ready for the convenient label *sentence.* The teacher merely notes that all the groups of words on the board that began with a capital letter and ended with a period are sentences. He also points out that each of the groups contains a word like *cat, dog, man,* or *woman* and a word like *walks, jumps,* or *talks.* If students give the traditional definition of a sentence, the teacher can merely accept it and move on to something else. He should not have students memorize the traditional definition.

Plural Nouns

The teacher writes these or other verbs on the board:

_____ run.   _____ talk.   _____ fly.

Again the teacher elicits responses by asking, "What things run, talk, or fly?" Sample responses may include:

| _____ run. | _____ talk. | _____ fly. |
| Cats run. | Boys talk. | Birds fly. |

Dogs run.	Girls talk.	Pigeons fly.
Horses run.	Students talk.	Robins fly.
Boys run.	Teachers talk.	Airplanes fly.
Men run.	Men talk.	Insects fly.
Women run.	Women talk.	Geese fly.
Children run.	Children talk.	Astronauts fly.

After students have filled the subject slots with a number of nouns, the teacher asks them how these nouns look alike. (Most end in -*s*. However, some words form their plurals by infixes, i.e., an internal change in the word. Examples: man-men, woman-women; foot-feet, goose-geese. Other words form their plurals by the addition of suffixes. Examples: child-children; ox-oxen.) Again the teacher asks students if they know what we call words like *cats, dogs, men, women, Russians,* and *Americans.* A majority of the students should remember the word *noun.* Then the teacher asks where the nouns appear in these sentences, and the students should note that in this pattern the noun always comes before a word like *walk, run, fly,* or *talk.* One student might note that such words are called verbs. If not, the teacher will mention the term and will use it from now on.

Is there a single word that students can place before the noun in each of the sentences written on the chalkboard? (the)

The airplanes fly.
The cats walk.
The dogs run.

Students should note that the word *the* is capitalized in the above responses since it comes first in the sentence.

Can students think of other words that they can place in front of all the plural nouns written on the chalkboard? Examples:

All airplanes fly.	Most airplanes fly.
These cats walk.	Two airplanes fly.
Those dogs run.	Many dogs run.
Their airplanes fly.	Few cats fly.
Some cats run.	Certain cats run.

Students should note that words like *the, all, most,* and *these* are called determiners because they signal that a noun is following.

FOR THE TEACHER ONLY. In *The Grammar of English Sentences,*[*] John Mellon presents this "master list" of determiners:

Pre-Article	Article	Demonstrative	Possessive
all	Ø	this	my
both	a(n)	that	our
only	the	these	your
	any	those	his
	every	some	her
	each	a certain	its
	some		their
	no		NOUN + -'s

(Note: the Ø or null sign simply indicates that no actual word is needed in the determiner position.)

Ordinal	Cardinal	Comparative
first	one	more
second	two	most such other
third	three	fewer
. . .	. . .	less
next	several	least
last	this many	
	that few	
	so much	
	too little	

It is not important for students to know the classes of determiners; however, it is important for them to see that certain words pattern with nouns and that such words are noun markers.

As students examine the plural nouns on the chalkboard, they should be able to add this item to what they already know about nouns: most nouns have both singular and plural forms and the plural form usually ends in *-s.*

*John C. Mellon, *The Grammar of English Sentences, Unit One.* Culver, Ind.: Culver Military Academy, 1963, p. 62.

What is the difference between the nouns preceding *walks* and those preceding *walk*? Which determiners pattern with plural nouns preceding *walk, run,* or *talk*? Have students suggest as many determiners as they can that precede plural nouns.

What generalization can students make by examining two lists like these?

The cat walks.	The cats walk.
This boy talks.	These boys talk.
An American runs.	Most Russians run.
The airplane flies.	All airplanes fly.
The girl jumps.	Most girls jump.

Students should be able to see that most singular nouns do not end in -*s* but that the verbs they precede do end in -*s* (in present tense). They should also see that most plural nouns end in -*s* and that the verbs they precede do not end in -*s* (in present tense).

Modification

To give their readers more information about cats, dogs, or airplanes, students can put other words in front of the nouns in the sentences they have written.

The _____ cats walk.
Question: What kind of cats?
Responses: The black cats walk.
The big black cats walk.

The teacher asks students to expand both the singular and plural noun phrases in the sentences written on the chalkboard. He asks each contributor to say the entire sentence and to write it in his notebook. The teacher also writes the complete sentence on the chalkboard.

What do students learn about the speaker if he says: "The green cats walk"? What change in the meaning of *cats* do students detect? What do students infer about cats and what do they learn about the speaker if he gives this sentence: "The cool cats walk"?

The teacher should explain, as the occasions arise in class, how words change meaning in time and context. He can find many excellent examples if he listens to students' conversations in the halls.

Students should have the opportunity to place adjectives before each of the nouns in the sentences on the board. What do they learn about adjectives? (Note: Students need not be troubled with the definition of adjective, and the teacher should use the term only as a convenient label.) Can adjectives stand alone in the noun slots? Can an adjective by itself pattern with *the*?

At this point it is probably better to have students use adjectives in the positive degree only and not trouble them with comparative and superlative degrees since the simple sentences written on the board are such that students will probably not use the comparative and superlative degrees. But if they should, the teacher should point out that adjectives can be readily detected because they are words that (a) can precede nouns, (b) cannot stand alone in the subject slot, (c) can have *-er* added to them or the word *more* placed in front of them to show comparison with two things, and (d) can have *-est* added to them or the word *most* placed in front of them to show comparison with three or more things.

In addition to their preceding nouns and not being able to stand alone in subject slots, adjectives also pattern with a group of words that traditional grammarians call adverbs and that linguists call intensifiers or qualifiers. Students need not be troubled with these terms, but they can readily see how adjectives pattern with intensifiers if the teacher asks, "How big are the black cats that walk?"

The *very* big black cats walk.
The *rather* big black cats walk.

(For the teacher: The most frequently used qualifiers or intensifiers are *very, rather, somewhat, quite, pretty, mighty, so, too, more, most, less,* and *least*. And, of course, there is the ever-present *real*, which might appear in a sentence like this: "The *real* cool cats walk." If it does, the teacher should not simply discard it as being substandard usage; he should take the occasion to talk about how language is used by various people and how the choice of words frequently marks a speaker more quickly than his clothing or manners.)

Which words can *very* precede? Do students understand that *very* is used correctly in the first sentence below and incorrectly in the second?

The very big black cats walk.
The very cats walk.

Do students know that *real*, which is sometimes used as an intensifier in informal usage, can also be used as an adjective?

The real cool cats walk.
Real airplanes fly.

Students should be led to see that many words can serve more than one function in a sentence. In the first sentence above the word *real* functions as an intensifier since it precedes the adjective *cool;* in the second sentence *real* functions as an adjective since it precedes the noun *airplanes.* It would probably be most unwise to belabor the point now, but it would not hurt to introduce the concept that words can work in various ways in sentences and that many words do not have fixed positions or slots into which they fit. This concept will be reinforced many times in later sentence patterns.

In addition to using adjectives and determiners, can students find other words, or groups of words, that can modify nouns? One method of expanding the noun, by adding prepositional phrases, can be brought out by writing a sentence like this on the chalkboard:

The black cats on _____ _____ walk.
The black cats on our street walk.
The black cats on our block walk.

All the boys in _____ _____ run.
All the boys in our class run.

The women behind _____ _____ talk.
The women behind our house talk.

Groups of words like *on our street, in our class,* and *behind our house* can be moved in the above sentences. If the teacher asks students to move those groups of words, these might be the results:

> The black cats walk on our street.
> All the boys run in our class.
> The women talk behind our house.

Can students detect the changes in meaning that are brought about by moving those groups of words? Can they see that both groups of sentences make perfect sense but that they do not mean the same thing? Can they see that simply by moving the groups of words like *on our street* and *behind our house* that they not only changed the structure of the sentences but that they also changed their meanings.

To reinforce some of the concepts presented thus far, the teacher will write a number of groups of words like these on the chalk-board:

> The _____ _____ _____ sing _____ _____ _____.
> The pretty little girls sing in the choir.
> All the _____ _____ girls _____ _____ _____ sing _____ _____
> choir.
> All the pretty little girls in our class sing in the choir.

Students should note that words like *girls* can precede the verb *sing*, and that girls can be modified by *all, the, pretty, little,* and *in our class.* Students should also be able to detect the difference in meaning between:

> All the pretty little girls in the choir sing on Sunday. (and)
> All the pretty little girls sing in the choir on Sunday.

By way of review students should be able to explain the changes in the nouns in the subject slots and in the verbs in groups of sentences like these:

> The pretty little girl sings in the choir on Sunday.
> All the pretty little girls sing in the choir on Sunday.

The big boy runs every Saturday. ...
All the big boys run every Saturday.

In each of the sentences above, which word fills the subject slot? What kind of word is it? How does the student know that it is a noun? Can he recall (a) that nouns are words like *cat*, *dog*, *man*, and *woman;* (b) that they are names that we give to classes of human beings, animals, or things; (c) that they are words that can be preceded by words like *a*, *an*, *the*, *every*, *this*, *that*, and *my;* (d) that they precede words like *walk, runs, talk*, and *jumps* in this sentence pattern; and (e) that nouns are words having two forms, a singular and a plural?

Students should also be familiar with the term *verb*, and they should know that words like *runs, walk, talks*, and *jump* function as verbs in the sentences they have been constructing. In the sentences written on the board, the verbs came after the noun subjects, and they were sometimes followed by groups of words like *in the choir*, *on our street*, and *in our class.*

A Backward Glance

Students should now realize that they can build sentences by starting with two basic words, a noun and a verb, and they can expand a two-word sentence into one containing a number of words. To show students what they have learned, the teacher will ask each student to select a plural noun like *cats*, *dogs*, *men*, *women*, or *airplanes* and a verb like *walk*, *run*, *talk*, *jump*, or *fly*. Starting with two of these words, students can build, by answering certain questions, sentences like these:

Boys run.
(Which boys run?)
All the boys run.
(What kind of boys?)
All the strong boys run.
(How strong are they?)
All the very strong boys run.
(How do they run?)
All the very strong boys run fast.
(Where do they run?)

All the very strong boys run fast around the track.
(When do they run?)
All the very strong boys run fast around the track after school.
(Are they all the strong boys in the school or in our class?)
All the very strong boys in our class run fast around the track
after school.

Starting with two words, a noun and a verb, the students were able to expand them into a long, albeit cumbersome, sentence. They should note that although they added a number of words to the sentence by answering the questions, the two words that they started with always remained in the same order: *boys* precedes *run*. In this first sentence pattern, then, many words can be added to the two basic words, the noun and the verb; but these two words always maintain the same relationship to one another: the noun precedes the verb. And these two words are the key words in the sentence. Without either of them, the basic or expanded sentences would not make sense. The teacher can demonstrate this by going back through the expansion above and by removing either the subject or the verb in each of the sentences.

Simple Tenses

Thus far we have been working with verbs in the present tense. To introduce the concept of time inherent in tenses of verbs and to give students more information about verbs, the teacher writes a part of a sentence like this on the chalkboard:

The cat _____ today.

The teacher asks students to fill the verb slot with as many different verbs as they can.* Each time they fill the verb slot, students read the entire sentence, not simply the verb. What do all the verbs have in common? (They all end in -*s*.)

*Note that students can also fill the slot with the past-tense form of a verb, e.g., The cat ate today. Thus, the teacher will need to limit the verbs to present-tense forms to introduce the concept of tense as it is presented here.

Then the teacher has students fill a verb slot like this with as many different verbs as they can.

The cats _____ today.

Students should note once again that the verbs in those two illustrations end in -*s* if the noun preceding them refers to only one animal, human, or thing, and that the verbs do not end in -*s* if the nouns that precede them do.

Next the teacher has students fill this verb slot with as many verbs as they can.

The cats _____ yesterday.

What do those verbs have in common? (Most end in -*ed*. The teacher may wish to put all the irregular verbs on a separate board for analysis later.)

Finally, the teacher has students fill this verb slot with as many different verbs as they can.

The cats _____ tomorrow.

How many words must students use to fill that verb slot? What do those verbs have in common?

Returning to the verbs that were used in the sentence containing the adverbial noun *today,* the teacher may note that all those verbs are in the present-tense form. Again students may be asked what characteristics present-tense forms of verbs have, and they may note that they have both singular and plural forms. Moving to the past-tense forms of the verbs, students should note that most of the verbs they used ended in -*ed*. When they wrote sentences containing the word tomorrow, the students returned to the present-tense form of the verb and put either shall or will in front of it. (Most students will use the auxiliary will; few will use shall. Slow learners, or any students for that matter, need not be troubled with the specious distinctions between shall and will.)

Just as *will* preceded verbs like *walk, talk, run,* or *jump,* other words can pattern with those verbs. (The teacher may wish to call such verbs auxiliaries, or he may simply say that such verbs work with other verbs.) To get students to use those verbs, the teacher may write a group of words like this on the board:

The black cats ———— walk on our street today.

The teacher asks the students to use as many words as they can with walk. Some sample responses are:

The black cats *can* walk on our street today.
The black cats *did* walk on our street today.
The black cats *may* walk on our street today.
The black cats *might* walk on our street today.
The black cats *could* walk on our street today.
The black cats *should* walk on our street today.
The black cats *will* walk on our street today.
The black cats *must* walk on our street today.

By removing the verb *walk* in each of the sentences above, the teacher should get students to see that words like *can* and *did* cannot stand alone in those sentences without another verb.

The teacher should ask students to explain the differences in meaning that result from the insertion of words like *can* and *did* in the above sentences.

By way of review, students should now understand (a) that a verb is one of the two most important words in a sentence; (b) that a verb always follows a noun in all the sentences that have been written on the chalkboard; (c) that verbs have different endings, i.e., *-s* in the present-tense singular and *-ed* or a change in the word in the past tense; (d) that verbs can pattern with words like *can, should, might, will,* and *did;* and (e) that verbs can be modified by words like *fast, today, tomorrow,* or by groups of words like *in the choir, in our class,* or *behind our house.*

To determine whether students are ready to move to the next sentence pattern, the teacher should give them several verbs that have not been used in sample sentences, and he should ask them to construct sentences like those that the class has been working on. Students should be able to start with a two-word sentence and expand it to include determiners, adjectives, adverbs, phrase modifiers, and auxiliary verbs.

SENTENCE PATTERN TWO—
$$N_S + V_{TR} + N_{OBJ}{}^*$$

As students worked with the first basic sentence pattern, they learned that the noun subject always precedes the verb. They also learned that determiners and adjectives precede nouns, that groups of words (prepositional phrases) can modify nouns and that these groups follow nouns, and that single words or groups of words can modify verbs and that such groups have great mobility. Without mentioning the concept, the teacher introduced students to word order. The teacher can now stress the importance of word order by introducing students to this second basic sentence pattern. He writes these words on the board:

the man   the boy   hit

If the teacher wrote the words like this:

The man the boy hit.

the students probably laughed since they do not utter sentences like that. The teacher then asks them to arrange the words in an order that makes sense. Students will probably give these two sentences:

The man hit the boy.
The boy hit the man.

The teacher should point out that although the words are identical in the two sentences, the meanings are definitely not the same. The changes in meaning result from the different ordering of the words. Although there are nouns on both ends of both sentences, the nouns do not function in the same way. The noun that precedes the verb is called the subject, just as *cats* was called the subject in "Cats walk"; the noun that follows the verb is called the object in this kind of sentence.

* Some teachers may find it easier to introduce this pattern as $N_1 + V_{tr} + N_2$. See page 26.

The teacher then writes groups of words like these on the board:

Mary bought a _____.
John threw the _____.
The little boy carried a _____.

The teacher asks students to fill the object slots with nouns and then to expand the sentences by using determiners, adjectives, adverbs, and groups of words that begin with words like *in*, *on*, and so forth. By this time they should be able to write sentences like these:

Yesterday Mary bought a watch in a department store in Junction City.
This morning John threw the old baseball over the fence into Mr. Johnson's yard.
The very little boy carried a sack of groceries home to his mother.

As students expand the sentences, the teacher should encourage them to use different determiners, a variety of adjectives, qualifiers, phrase modifiers, and auxiliary verbs.

What do students learn about word order in this particular sentence pattern? (No matter how they expand a sentence, the basic order, noun-verb-noun, does not change.)

Pronouns

As the teacher wrote "the man the boy hit" on the board, the students saw that the words needed to be arranged in a definite order to make sense. Yet the words themselves do not give a clue to this arrangement. The two noun phrases are identical in structure, and they can be arranged in sentences like these, depending on the meaning intended:

The man hit the boy.
The boy hit the man.

Since nouns are not inflected to show their function in a sentence, word order is the only clue. With this pattern, we can introduce pronouns whose form and position indicate their function in a sentence.

To introduce pronouns, the teacher may write groups of words like these on the board:

1. the man the boy hit
2. the man him hit
3. the man the boy hit
4. him he hit

Students should see that the first group of words can be arranged to read:

The man hit the boy. (or)
The boy hit the man.

Since the noun phrases are identical, the word order indicates only the meaning desired. However, with the second group of words, students should have little trouble arranging them in this order:

The man hit him.

In this sentence, the word *him* is the key to the arrangement. Students will need to see that *him* is a pronoun, i.e., a word that can stand in place of a noun, and that this particular form can be used only as the object in a sentence, not the subject. To illustrate how pronouns replace nouns, the teacher can return to a sentence like "The man hit the boy," and have students assume that the boy referred to is in the class. If they were saying the sentence in the class, they probably would not say "The man hit the boy," but "The man hit him." In substituting *him* for *boy*, the students would either point to the boy or would have a preceding sentence that would be explicit enough so that all readers or listeners would understand who the *him* is.

Next the teacher has students work with groups of words like 3 and 4 above. Students rearrange "The man the boy hit" to be either "The boy hit the man" or "The man hit the boy." Students should assume that both the boy and the man are close enough so that they can be pointed to or referred to in some specific manner.

If they were to take the fourth group of words then, they would say, "He hit him." Here the forms of the pronouns are such that they must come in this order. He is the subject and him is the object. Students, even slow-learning students, do not say, "Him hit he." Students should consider the problems of using these two pronouns in this one sentence. Going back to the two possible sentences—"The boy hit the man" or "The man hit the boy"—students should see clearly that we can tell by the arrangement who hit whom. But if we were to substitute, without giving them the original sentences, "He hit him," could they tell whether the boy or the man was hit unless more specific information were given or unless the speaker pointed to each person as he used the pronouns *he* and *him?*

Like all students, slow learners have a tendency to overuse pronouns without giving specific references. The teacher should emphasize that since pronouns substitute for nouns the speaker must be specific enough in his sentences so that the listener or reader will know definitely to whom the pronoun refers.

At this stage it would probably be wise to introduce only these pronouns to students:

I	we	you	he	she	it	they
me	us	you	him	her	it	them

Students should construct as many sentence patterns as they can using the second basic pattern, $N_s V_{tr} N_{obj}$, and they should expand these sentences by using determiners, adjectives, qualifiers, and phrase modifiers. Wherever possible, the teacher should note that a pronoun could be substituted for either the noun subject or the noun object if the listener or reader can determine from the total context to whom the pronoun refers. The teacher should work with students on substituting pronouns for nouns, and without referring to case or without emphasizing the terms subject and object, the teacher can drill students on pronoun use in this sentence pattern. Sentences like these might help:

Mary bought a watch.
Mary bought it.

She bought it. (Does the reader know to whom and to what
she and it refer?)
Mary got the groceries.
Mary got them.
She got them. (Does the reader know to whom and to what
she and them refer?)
_____ threw the ball.
_____ threw _____.
(How many different pronouns can students put in each of the
above subject slots? How many pronouns can they put in the
object slots? If they say, "He threw it," do they know to whom
and to what the pronouns refer?)

Review

The teacher will give students an opportunity to make as many
sentences as they can with sentence pattern two. He should encourage students to use the three simple tenses, to expand nouns
and verbs through modification, and to substitute pronouns wherever such substitution is feasible.

At this point students should see that nouns can either be the
subject or the object in a sentence and that the noun's function as
either of these depends entirely upon word order, not upon changes
in the form of the word.

The Passive Transformation*

By rearranging the noun subject and the noun object in the
second basic sentence pattern, students can construct passive re-
orderings of their sentences. They need not be troubled with the
terms passive and reordering, but they should see that sentence
pattern two suggests several possibilities. To go back to an already
overworked sentence, "The boy hit the man," students can rear-

---

*Some teachers may wish to teach this transformation much later in the
program, but it can be taught at this point without confusing students.

range the order by a simple transposition of elements and by a simple insertion of several words. For example:

The boy hit the man. (becomes)
The man was hit by the boy.

Given several sentences like those above, students should be able to tell, in their own words, how the second sentence is formed. This reordering will also help fix the concepts of subject and object in their minds, since, in the reordering, they must take the object and make it the subject. They might even arrive at a formula like this for rearranging the elements:

object + is, are, was, or were + verb (past participle) + by + subject

Students should note that the noun that did function as the object now functions as the subject, and the noun that did function as the subject now comes after the word *by*.

Students should again construct their own sentences using the second sentence pattern and then rearrange the sentences so that the objects become the subjects. They should write sentences like these on the chalkboard so that they can examine enough evidence to make generalizations:

John threw the ball.
The ball was thrown by John.
The car passed the truck.
The truck was passed by the car.
The pretty little girl sang "Stardust."
"Stardust" was sung by the pretty little girl.

By introducing this passive transformation, the teacher introduces students to the third principal part of the verb. In working with simple tenses, students learned (a) that verbs are words like *talk, walk, jump,* and *fly;* (b) that they have both singular and plural forms in the present tense; (c) that they add *-ed* or change internally to indicate past time; (d) that they come after noun subjects in the sentences written on the chalkboard; and (e) that they can be modified by words like *fast, today,* or *this morning,* or by groups of words like *in our class, in the choir,* or *behind the house.* With the passive transformation, students become acquainted with another means of identifying verbs. Added to their knowledge is the fact that verbs have a third form, the past participle (which they need not know by name), which helps in their identification. Verbs, then, are those words which do everything indicated above plus fit into a paradigm like this:

walk	walks	walked	walked	walking
sing	sings	sang	sung	singing
fly	flies	flew	flown	flying
throw	throws	threw	thrown	throwing

SENTENCE PATTERN THREE— $N_{SUBJ} + V_{TR} + N_{IO} + N_{OBJ}$*

To introduce the third basic sentence pattern, the teacher writes groups of words like these on the chalkboard:

My father gave _____ a watch.
Mary told the _____ the truth.
The well-dressed man left the _____ a ten-dollar tip.

As students fill those slots, they should see that they can use either nouns or pronouns. Questions like, "To whom did my father give the watch?" or "To whom did Mary tell the truth?" might help students understand what nouns and pronouns in this position do. Students should also construct a number of sentences using this pattern, and they should have the opportunity to fill the slots in a number of sentences like those above that have either been prepared by the teacher or by students. Students should note that nouns or pronouns in this position normally come directly after the verb. They should also note the form of the pronoun that they must use here. Filling the slots with pronouns only should get them in the habit of using the proper form. They should also see that pronouns,

---

*Some teachers may wish to use these symbols: $N_1 + V_{tr} + N_2 + N_3$.

unlike nouns, cannot be preceded by determiners. Therefore, they cannot put *her* into the indirect object slot in this sentence, "The well-dressed man left the ____ a ten-dollar tip," without removing the determiner *the*.

After students have filled a number of indirect object slots with nouns or pronouns and after they have constructed a number of their own sentences using this pattern, the teacher may wish to give them the convenient label, *indirect object*.

Sentences with indirect objects can be restated like this:

My father gave a watch to Mary.
Mary told the truth to the principal.
The well-dressed man left a ten-dollar tip for the waiter.

Students should be told that the words Mary, principal, and waiter are no longer indirect objects but nouns that function in the phrases, *to Mary, to the principal,* and *for the waiter.* The only reason for restating the sentence like this is to give slow learners another means of identifying sentences of this pattern. If they can take the noun or pronoun that immediately follows the verb and receives the object, and if they can put it at the end of a sentence in a group of words that begins with *to* or *for,* then they know that they have a sentence that contains an indirect object.

By this time students have learned that nouns can fill a number of slots in sentences. They should note that in this sentence pattern, for example, nouns can fill three slots: the subject, the indirect object, and the object. And in each case, the nouns can be preceded by determiners and adjectives with their qualifiers, and nouns can be followed by groups of words that begin with words like *in* or *on.* Thus, starting with a sentence like "Mary told the principal the truth," students can expand the nouns in the sentence like this:

A very timid Mary told the most understanding principal of our school the ugly truth about the incident in the gymnasium.

The Passive Transformation

Like sentence pattern two, sentence pattern three can be re-ordered by this formula:

indirect object + was + verb (past participle) + object + by + subject

Following that formula, a sentence like "My father gave Mary a watch" becomes

Mary was given a watch by my father.

Reordering the sentences gives slow-learning students another way of saying the same sentence and also helps them become more familiar with terms like subject, indirect object, and object, since they must remove these elements from the original sentence and place them in different positions in the reordered sentences. However, if this step seems to confuse students, it would be wise to ignore it for the time being.

SENTENCE PATTERN FOUR—
$N_{SUBJ} + V_{LI} + N_{COMP}$ (OR ADJ)*

The teacher writes groups of words like these on the chalkboard:

Mary is a _____.
The airplane is a _____.
The man in the dark suit is a_____.

Students should fill the slots in sentences like those with as many words as they can. What kind of words fit here? Students should note that only nouns fit in those slots since each of the illustrative sentences has a determiner *a*, which signals that a noun is following.

After students have filled a number of predicate nominative slots (the term is not necessary for students to know), they should be asked to expand the nouns in this position by adding qualifiers, adjectives, and groups of words that follow nouns and begin with

---

*Some teachers may wish to use these symbols: $N_1 + V_{11} + \begin{cases} N_2 \\ Adj. \end{cases}$
See page 26.

words like *in* or *on*. Students may come up with expansions like these:

> Mary is a very pretty little girl in the seventh grade.
> The airplane is a mighty jet with swept-back wings.
> The man in the dark suit is the president of the Olympic Manufacturing Company.

Only a few verbs can be used in this sentence pattern. To illustrate the small number, the teacher can put groups of words like these on the chalkboard, have students fill the predicate nominative slots, and then call attention to these verbs, noting that these verbs appear in sentences with nouns that follow verbs and that give us more information about the subject.

> I am a _____.
> The man is a _____.
> The engineers are the _____.
> The man was a _____.
> The dogs were the _____.
> The ice cream will be a _____.
> The school became a _____.
> The man had been a _____.

Thus far students have learned (a) that nouns are words like *cat, dogs, man,* and *engineers,* (b) that they have both singular and plural forms, (c) that they can be preceded by determiners and adjectives, (d) that they can be followed by groups of words that begin with words like *in* and *on,* (e) that they can fill subject, object, and indirect object slots in the sentence patterns covered thus far, and (f) that when they function as subjects they precede the verbs in these sentence patterns. Now students have another means of identifying nouns. A noun is any word whose singular form can fit a test pattern like this:

> "This is a(n) _____."

In this particular pattern, the verb can be followed by a noun, pronoun, or adjective. To illustrate the use of the adjective, the teacher writes groups of words like these on the board:

The girl is _____.
The little dog is _____.
The airplane is _____.

The teacher asks students to fill the slots with as many different adjectives as they can. One additional method of determining whether a word is an adjective is by putting it in this test slot: "This seems _____."

By this time students have learned that adjectives are words (a) that can modify nouns, (b) that can be preceded by words like *very, somewhat,* and *rather,* and (c) that can fill the test slot, "This seems _____."

As was indicated earlier, students have been working primarily with adjectives in the positive degree. Now comparative and superlative degrees can be introduced with groups of words like these:

Mary is tall.
Mary is _____ than Jane.
Mary is the _____ girl in the class.
Sylvester is intelligent.
Sylvester is _____ _____ than John.
Sylvester is the _____ _____ boy in the class.

After filling a number of slots with adjectives in the comparative and superlative degrees, students should see that they have another means of identifying adjectives. Adjectives are words to which students can add -*er* or precede by the word *more* to compare two things, and to which they can add -*est* or precede by the word *most* to compare three or more things.

Adverbial Elements

After mastering the concepts presented in the first four basic sentence patterns, slow-learning students can begin studying the material presented in the approach for academically talented and average students if the teacher continues to use the approach explained in this essay. For example, the teacher might approach the section on adverbial elements (see page 40) like this:

> When we started working with sentence pattern one, we found that a basic sentence consisting of only three words does not give us as much information as we might want. For example:
>
> The boy slept.

We might want to know when he slept, or where he slept, or how he slept. In other words, we want to supply different words for these underscored words (shown in italics below) on the chalkboard:

> The boy slept *sometime.*
> The boy slept *somewhere.*
> The boy slept *somehow.*

What words can we substitute for *sometime*? (The teacher asks volunteers to write complete sentences on the chalkboard and also asks students to write complete sentences in their notebooks.) Then the teacher asks students to substitute other words or phrases for *somewhere* and *somehow*. Next the teacher introduces the concepts presented in the rest of the section on adverbial elements using the approach described in this essay.

SLOW LEARNERS AND SYNTAX

Several teachers in the pilot schools learned that their slow-learning students could master many of the concepts presented in the approach for academically talented and average students if the teacher presented the material slowly, explained it thoroughly, and encouraged students to build, not analyze, sentences. The teachers further learned that slow learners could master the concepts if they were permitted to arrive at their own definitions of terms and if teachers did not emphasize terminology. All of the material presented in the approach for academically talented and average students from page 40 on can be presented to slow-learning students in a modified form and at a much slower pace than is suggested for their more talented classmates if the "approach is right." As one pilot-school teacher commented:

> Perhaps the most helpful unit was "Teaching the Basic Sentence Patterns to Slow-learning Students." Each student became actively involved in his observation of sentences on the chalkboard and then with his writing, reordering, and expanding sentences in his notebook. Incidentally, I highly recommend the use of a notebook because, simultaneously, sentence sense, spelling, punctuation, capitalization, and handwriting can be steadily improved without confusing the slow student with rules and traditional jargon. Also, the notebook serves as a storehouse and a record of progress. However, an important feature of this unit is that the sentence pattern symbols stimulate interest in non-academic students. To be able to discuss a sentence pattern N V N N made them feel ten feet tall. When a class of under-privileged students with I.Q.'s averaging about 85 got excited about the basic structure of the English language, I, too, felt ten feet tall. Slow students *can* learn if the method is right. For the first time in forty years of experience have I had any degree of success in teaching slow learners sentence structure.